WOMEN'S ROLE IN THE 20th CENTURY MANIPUR

WOMEN'S ROLE IN THE 20th CENTURY MANIPUR

A Historical Study

Mrs. Tingneichong G. Kipgen

KALPA

Women's Role in the 20th Century Manipur : A Historical Study

Rs. 540

ISBN: 978-81-7835-803-1

Published in 2010 in India by
Kalpaz Publications
C-30, Satyawati Nagar,
Delhi-110052
E-mail: kalpaz@hotmail.com
Phone : 9212729499

Laser Type Setting by: Rudra Computer Graphics, Delhi
Printed at : Chawla Offset Printers, Delhi

Contents

	Foreword	7
	Preface	9
	Acknowledgements	13
1.	**Introduction**	15
2.	**Meitei Women's Role** • Meitei Women's Role in Society • Meitei Women' Role in Economy • Meitei Women's Role in Politics • Meitei Women's Role in Religion.	23
3.	**Meitei Pangal Women's Role** • Meitei Pangal Women's Role in Society • Meitei Pangal Women's Role in Politics • Meitei Pangal Women's Role in Economy. • Meitei Pangal Women's Role in Religion.	49
4.	**Kuki Women's Role** • Kuki Women's Role in Society • Kuki Women's Role in Politics • Kuki Women's Role in Economy • Kuki Women's Role in Sports • Kuki Women's Role in Religion • Kuki Women's Role in Church.	79
5.	**Naga Women's Role** • Naga Women's Role in Society • Naga Women's Role in Politics • Naga Women's Role in Economy	123

• Naga Women's Role in Religion • Naga Women's Role in Church.

6. Women and Health **155**

7. Conclusion **165**

Bibliography **173**

Index **191**

Foreword

It is my pleasure to write a brief foreword to this book by Mrs. Tingneichong Kipgen.

The roles of women in Manipur has been discussed and debated in the various academic forums till date. Published books on the roles of Manipuri Women belonging to different communities are very few. Considering the need in this direction, I believe the book will be of immense help to the students, research scholars and users.

I wish her all success in" her endeavour and sincerely hope that the readers will appreciate the book.

(O. Landhoni Devi)
MLA, 35-Khangabok A/C.

Preface

Society is progressing in every field, be it in politics, economy, religion, and also women's role in these aspects. This study tries to bring out the roles of women in every field in order to present their roles as catalyst in the development process. In order to understand the roles played by women in Manipur we feel the need to examine women from the traditional to the modern context. Progressive modernization brought by the spread of education gradually altered the situation, and women in Manipur have begun to participate in diverse modern activities. They began to venture out of homes and their awareness of oneself and society is increasing. This work also tries to reflect that the trend is from ascribed status to an achieved one and that women's role is not limited to the home as was in the traditional society.

Women studies have kindled interest all over the world due to increased public awareness and academic interest.

This study is also carried out to understand the importance of the role played by women in society, religion, politics and economy. Their roles are very important because women in Manipur entered into the 21st century with many changes taking place in their societies some for good and some not so good. This study has been carried out to take advantages of the changes for growth, prosperity and to keep on developing with the changes. This study also incorporates the contemporary events which have a direct bearing on the socio-economic and political life of the women.

As all necessary materials are not found in the books alone, attempts have been made to uncover information based on primary sources like field work, personal interviews, both formal and informal discussions with knowledgeable persons. Stories of past events from the mouth of the elders constitute no less important a source as it helps the researcher to understand the history of the roles of women played especially among the Kuki and the Naga women.

Journals, Newspaper, Magazines, souvenirs, unpublished books, documents (in tribal dialect), memorandum, booklets, dissertations, etc. written in English and vernaculars which have little or direct bearing on my research topic are also considered within the sources of my study.

Secondary sources which itself is dependent on primary sources are being the major references for quotations and to derive new interpretation and hypothesis. The findings of others are also brought together in support of my own hypothesis. This work will give basic ideas of women belonging to different communities in a complete form.

Therefore, we may state that women of Manipur have achieved much and their work participation rate is also very high. Yet, these achievements have not enabled these women to break the tentacles of patriarchy and enter the decision making channels to subscribe legislation rights in their favour.

The basic objective of the proposed topic is therefore to study the development of women's role not as an isolated instance but as an essential part of Manipur's problematic entry into modernity. The scope of the study which is to trace the growth of dominant discourses on women from the early twentieth century to the present.

Introduction

The roles of Meitei women.

The roles of Meitei Pangal Women.

The roles of Kuki women.

The roles of Naga women.

The importance of Women and Health

Conclusion.

Acknowledgements

As I write this acknowledgement, I want to thank God for His blessing during the course of my research work.

My first and foremost deepest gratitude are due to my supervisor, Dr. Salam Irene, Associate Professor, Department of History, Manipur University. She has guided me with a lot of patience and understanding. Her valuable guidance, direction and encouragement are the stepping stone without which I would not have completed my work in time. Despite my illness, various weaknesses and limitations which at time did intervene to restrict my progress, she has endured with patience and persuaded me to go on; for this I am forever indebted to her.

Secondly, I owe my gratitude to the faculty members of the Department of History, Manipur University for their help and encouragement.

Thirdly, I would like to acknowledge my gratitude to the entire staff of the Manipur University Library, Imphal, Tribal Research Centre, Imphal and various authors whose works quoted at the appropriate places inside the Thesis help me to undertake the present research in a more objective and logical way.

Last but not the least, I am also deeply grateful to my children and husband for their patience, encouragement and for their prayers. My husband's understanding and encouragement was the real source of strength especially in times of strain and stress.

Tingneichong G. Kipgen

1

Introduction

India has a history which goes back to approximately 500 B.C. But the history of women's movement in India begins much later in the last decades of the 19th century. Interest in women's issues was initiated by the male intelligentsia of this period. In India women live and grow up in a male dominated society. In the pre-colonial period as well as under the colonial rule, the traditional role of women was to be subservient to men. They were not considered part of civil society and were deprived of their rights. Historically, the British conquest of India did not bring any radical change in Indian society and especially in the position of women. It was observed by the East India Company and later by the Crown that any interference in society would be regarded as an encroachment on indigenous religion and social customs and may jeopardize colonial rule. The Government of India in 1975 by forming "Committee on Status of Women" took up issues relating to women. Different approaches are adopted to examine the position and status of women in any given social structure.

The preamble to the Constitution of India declares equality of status and provides equal opportunities to all citizens, thereby making no difference between men and women. Article 14 ensures 'Equality before law' and article 15 prohibits any discrimination. Article 15(3) empowers the state to 'any special provision for women and children'. State policy of the Directive Principles in Part IV of the Indian Constitution pays concern to women directly and has a special bearing on their status. Article 39(a) provides Right to an adequate means of livelihood for men and women. But most of the women could not enjoy the benefits of the Articles of the Constitution due to tradition bound social evils in the society.

Despite constraints, women are passing through a stage of social change.

Indigenous people of Manipur are composed of a number of ethnic communities and tribes in the plain and hills of Manipur. Women in tribal areas enjoyed more freedom of movement compared to their counterparts in the valley. The evils of the dowry system and purdah system does not plague the society. Generally, in the tribal society, divorce is allowed but rarely practiced. No restriction is imposed on the life of the widow in regard to their food, clothes etc., as it is found in the case of a widow from a Hindu family. A widow is allowed to marry again. The "bride price" custom among the tribals or tribes in Manipur does not appear to have attracted the evils of the usual dowry system. But mobility of people from other states, interaction and intermixing of Customs and affluence of some families led to dowry in some cases among the Meitei society.

The economic dependence of women on men is an acknowledged reason for the low status of women. Women have to work hard; sadly their work remains invisible and marginal. Women's physical labour which remains invisible is not counted as work.

Meitei women are not only major economic contributors but they also have a considerable voice in the political sphere. Manjusri Chaki Sircar has remarked in her book "Feminism in a Traditional Society" that in Manipur Valley, the process of Sanskritization failed to work in the socio-economic and religious areas because of the vital presence of female power, which may be described as a kind of feminism. This can be recognized in women's individual self-reliance and collective solidarity". The rapid increase in the number of English medium schools and also the increased number of girl students show the concern of parents for better education of their children. The impact of education is seen in the life style and size of the family.

Education is considered a potent instrument through which the process of modernization of the society could be affected. Now-a-days, in all the communities of Manipur, it is found that girls prefer to select their own life-partners and educated girls are interested in securing jobs to attain not only economic independence but to live a life free from economic difficulties. It is true that working women suffer from role conflict in a conservative society and traditional family set up. Working women have to bear unbearable burdens in the form of physical and mental strains in discharging duties at home and in jobs. There are instances of the husband's denial of the right of the wife over her own earned money or her privileges and obligations but such a situation has been changed to a large extent due to education of women. Many educated women try to assert themselves in different situations. Education gives women mental strength and self confidence to face problems in life.

Unfortunately, illiteracy of adults especially of women stands as a stumbling block in all developmental programmes for which so much importance has been laid in Adult Education Programme, Non-Formal and Informal programmes.

In Manipur, women always played an important role in all spheres of life. (The state is a home to a large number of ethnic groups, including 29 scheduled tribes.) Historical reasons greatly influenced the independent growth of these social groups with varying degrees of cultural development and civilization of whom the Meiteis are the most dominant and advanced nationality.

The tribe-people, who live in a predominance position, are greatly influenced by the linguistic and cultural affinities between the Meiteis and hill-tribes of Manipur and their folk-lore.

The Meitei Pangal also settled in Manipur since 17th century and adopted the Meitei language as their mother tongue and now form an integral part of the Manipuri society. In Manipur, social harmony which is the basic requirement of a society is maintained by Manipuris unspoiled and unbroken.

Social progress is closely linked with the role women play in society. It would be impossible to discuss the past, the present and the future of humanity without dwelling on the role played by women. Women play a greater role in society that we are aware of. From early period women have dominated a role or a part in the affairs of the society, from the smallest level in the form of a family to the biggest circle of influencing the development of the state.

Due to the influence of various religions like Hinduism, Islam and Christianity which came to Manipur during different period of times in history, which brought in their taboos and belief, the status enjoyed by women of Manipur deteriorated. Still, despite this regression, the position of women in Manipur remained much better than elsewhere in India.

The political participation of women had completely transformed their nature and pattern of life. The shy domesticated and inferior women gave way to bold, strong and confident women engaged in the public sphere. Fortunately, modern changes are taking place in a transitional phase in the societies of Manipur. "Many women have attempted to develop their lives by drawing power through external sources of financial support polity and society. Others however, have tried to sustain strength and confidence by seeking a spiritual path as well. The spirituality of women today remains a relatively uncharted area. The scholarly literature is confined to religious aspects of women's lives, rules, roles and rituals of women in various religions, superstitious behaviour, myths and symbolic representations in art, sculpture, dance, music, cinema, television and literature or to research on religious practitioners such as Yogis, gurus and renunciants".[1]

This research work also presents a sociological study of modern secular women for the purpose of understanding the nature of their roles in society, politic, economy and religion.

When academicians and activists highlight the "scarcity syndrome" experienced by a majority of the ignored and marginalized rural women in India – their struggle to procure the most basic necessities of life such as food, fuel and water, their minimal control over the conditions and the products of their labour; their passive role in the decision making process within the family – one may then wonder about the spirit that keeps these women alive and ticking. To many urban women, the positive realities of rural life and the well springs of their strength remain hidden.[2]

The roles played by women in Manipur in different walks of life are the greatest social fabric of Manipur.

Manipuri Women played an important role in the productive process of the state and they are guardians of the state, always on the forefront defending human rights. The emergence of Meira Paibis or Women Torch Bearers in Manipur is a revolutionary phenomenon.

In order to bring out the various roles played by the women of Manipur it is necessary to study the roles played by women belonging to different communities, because each community has its own social order that influences women by and large. They preserved their culture and social order upto certain extent inspite of the influence of Christianity, Hinduism and Islam. Though there are vast differences in their life styles and social structures, there are considerable similarities too. The high status accorded to her womenfolk is one of the prides of Manipur. As their roles widened they are mentally, intellectually and morally equipped to tackle problems of state, terrorism, violence, conflicting problems between state and insurgents.

Women in Manipur have sustained a distinct tradition of female guardianship within a predominantly male dominated society. Their participation in various social causes and religious ceremonies that are central to the cultural ethos of Manipuri society show that patriarchal discourses however, perpetuating, evidently do not always succeed in drowning women out. Women in Manipur are always in the forefront of various social and political movements. Pandit Jawaharlal Nehru aptly remarked that "To awaken the society it is the women who must be awakened. Once she is on the move the family moves; the village moves and the nation moves".

The health infrastructure also needs attention and improvement and there is a necessity of conducting health awareness drives. There is an increasing realization among women that incentives have to be provided to help women overcome their backwardness in almost all spheres.

References

1. An exploration of the spirituality of urban Indian Women by Renuka Singh, Penguin Books; p. 1.
2. See towards equality – Report of the Committee on Status of Women in India, 1974, ICSSR, Department of Human Welfare, New Delhi.

2

Role of Meitei Women

(I) THE ROLE OF MEITEI WOMEN IN SOCIETY

Meitei women have a distinctively higher position and status with greater responsibilities than women of other societies. Mrs. Grimwood in her book "My three years in Manipur" has said that "Manipuris do not shut up their women, as is the custom in most parts of India and they are much more enlightened and intelligent in consequences"[1].

Meitei women have inherited social responsibilities in different forms and in a changed situation. According to E.W. Dun "they are very industrious; in this respect the opposite of the men who are lazy and indolent. Most of the works of the country, except the heaviest, are performed by them and they are consequently the main stay of the family circle. All the marketing is done by women and all the work of buying and selling in public, and the carrying to and fro of the articles to be sold; whilst at home they are busily employed in weaving and spinning. It would be difficult to find a more industrious woman in India than the Manipuri.[2]

There are different categories of women having different characters in the mythology of Manipur. Characters like Panthoibi, Emoinu and Phouoibi etc. shows that Meitei women are bold, courageous, independent and enjoy their due rights and have an honourable place in the society. Their characters have played a great influence on the present day Meitei women of Manipur in their family, social, economic and political lives. Many educated Meitei women are observing traditional norms and practices in their homes and at the same time discharging their respective duties and responsibilities at their work places.

According to Prof. M.C. Arun, women in the family is a submissive individual bound by a number of patriarchal manacles and on the other hand a woman in the market is a unit of forceful collectivity. This peculiar relation between the individual self and collectivity is because of the unique historical experience of the Meitei society that had emerged out of a series of ethnic amalgamation.[3]

It is a fact that "the worshipping of goddesses was started from ancient period in Manipur".[4]

The position of women in a subordinate status started with the coming of Hinduism in Manipur. But inspite of the strong ideological impact of Hindu Brahmanas, Meitei women have retained their important roles in the society. The majority of women still continue to perform traditionally assigned gendered roles. Individuals, as members of the families form a society. The social relationship between members of the different families is mainly conducted through women. All domestic works in the family are performed by the women irrespective of their class or status. Meitei women usually take the responsibility for the maintenance of the family. In addition to her household duties, she has to participate in the social functions of their localities, or join the "Meira Paibi"s. It is the local Meira Paibis who are playing a most significant role for the protection of human rights of the people of the state.

They keep a constant vigil day and night against any possible or actual violation of human conduct and rights of their respective localities. These women are quick to point out that they are mothers, sisters and wives. And, as such, they cannot remain indifferent when the human rights of their social members get seriously endangered.

Meitei women were brave and courageous. It can be seen even in the 17th Century from the example of Pithetleima (1652-1666) who was the mother of King Paikhomba who ruled after Kind Khunjaoba fought the enemy in the absence of the King and went for an expedition at Tangda Village. After the expedition she came to be known as Tangdakhombi or Tangjakhombi.[5]

Pithetleima ruled after King Khunjaoba as he had no heir.[6]

Luckily, the age-old tradition of exercising restraint so as not to inflict physical harm to women at least in the public have also worked in their favour.

As time goes by their status as human rights activists have increased tremendously. The "Meira Paibi"s play a vital role in the context of the Meitei society, not only in their unending attempts to sustain a sense of moral superiority amongst the people of Manipur, but also in their assertion of their domestic relevance in a politically sensitive region.

Therefore, "Meira Paibi"s have become a new political force that challenges the state and its apparatuses for curtailing human freedom and dignity as well as encroaching upon individual liberty. The "Meira Paibi"s from 1980 onwards changed their role from being Nasha Bandhis to that of Meira Paibis (torch bearers). According to Prof. Ksh. Bimola Devi, "The social life of Manipur during the last two and half decades was dominated by Dharnas, sit-in-protests, demonstrations, rallies, etc. organized by the Meira Paibis in every nook and corner of Manipur. The movement was mainly against the injustice meted out by the state authority, against excesses committed by the security personnel, against violation of human rights, etc. The Meira Paibis are also actively associated in the movement for the protection of territorial integrity of Manipur in June, July 2001 and other subsequent programmes launched by social organizations like AMUCO (All Manipur United Organisation), UCM (United Committee Manipur) and other like-minded organizations. Among the women who sacrificed their lives and inspired the minds of the people of Manipur were Pyari, who died in 1986 and Th. Monorama, whose dead body was found abandoned in the next morning of her arrest in 2004. The name of Irom Chanu Sharmila stands distinct for fighting against injustice committed against the innocent civilians by the security forces.[7] When situation compelled then women came out as soldiers and fight the enemy courageously".[8]

For instance, the latest disrobing of 12 women Meira Paibis in front of the gates of the Assam Rifles in July 2004 as a non-violent mark of protest against the rape and killing of their fellow member Monorama Devi caught the imagination of those who take cursory interest in justice.

Motherly roles of women to look after the welfare of her children, their performance in schools and socialization are spheres in which women play important roles. The situation of conflict and women's engagement in other social activities sometimes greatly affect these responsibilities, which sometimes led to a number of school drop-outs, tendency to join armed-opposition groups among teenagers, taking drugs etc.

In the development of the society, the role of women in the society cannot be ignored as women constituted half of the population of the society.

In Meitei society, there is no strict separation of the sexes in everyday life. They sit together on several festive occasions. This can be seen during the eleven days of Rath Jatra festival, where men and women clap and dance together by singing 'Khubak Isei'. Meitei women show adaptability to different environments and to team up for social and economic survival. Thus, they enjoy a social bond through recreational activities.

In Meitei society, dowry system was absent. However, with the influence of Hinduism, the dowry system became quite predominant. Even though it was not mandatory for the parents to give dowry many economically well to do parents have induced themselves to offering heavy dowries for their daughters in the present state. In Meitei society, it is believed that the concept of dowry has its source in 'Laisemlon Ariba Puja' which mentioned the giving of 'A-oon-pot' as early as 1500 BC.[9]

According to Prof. Gangmumei "with the conversion into Hinduism, some ideals of Hindu women hood had been inculcated. The first instance of Sati burning was in the year 1725 AD when a prince named Murari died his two wives volunteered to be burned along with their husband. The second instance was in 1733 AD; one Khurairakpa of Sapam family died at Chinga and his wife dies along with him. A Brahmin's two wives committed Sati in the same year. Most of these burnings were in the reign of Garibniwas. During the time of Bheigyachandra, it appears that Sati burning was no longer popular."[10]

In the Meitei society, parents always adopt equal attitude and behaviour towards their sons and daughters. Even though preference is given to boys, there is no girl-child infanticide.

With the coming of modernity in the society, changes in attitude, behaviour, and dress can be seen in the family lifestyles.

Towards the close of the 20th Century among the Meitei women a class called Elite women of Manipur emerges. We have women who excel in sports – weight lifting (Kunjarani); in boxing; in the field of art and culture; education, business administrations, doctors, engineers etc. In any field they put their heart and mind, Meitei women can do it and will become fore runners and be an example to other women belonging to different societies of Manipur and the world.

(II) THE MEITEI WOMEN'S ROLE IN ECONOMY

Meitei women take major part in the economic life of the state in which they enjoy maximum independence. Women in Meitei society are believed to be of divine origin and culturally esteemed as the defenders of social tranquility. They make crucial economic contribution and hold a distinctive position in social, religious and political life.

"The process of Sanskritisation failed to work in the social economic and religious areas because of the vital presence of female power which may be described as a kind of feminism".[11]

Meitei women on the whole are docile and submissive, but on any social issues they are assertive at collective level. In a Meitei proverb it is said "a man who does not go to Loisang and a woman who does not go to the market both are worthless".[12]

Historically, Meitei women's role widened after the Seven Years devastation. The devastation of the male population in the Seven Years war made her to take up the responsibility of trade and economic activities. Moreover, the advent of colonialism in 1891 integrated Manipur to a wider capitalist system and improved transportation network enabled them to extend their trading activities beyond Manipur.

According to B. Kulachandra Singh "while the Pacha Loishang and women's right to appeal have disappeared over the time, the institution of keithel and women's economic role have persisted amidst the rising hardships. Women also continued to perform traditionally assigned gendered roles such as domestic chores and weeding during paddy season. Subsequent integration of Manipur has not altered the roles of women".[13]

Since agriculture is the main occupation of the people of Manipur, women participated equally with men in cultivation work and also at the time of harvesting. In the fields women work in teams known as "Khutlang" on payment of money in exchange of work. Sometimes they work as hired labours in order to earn extra income. The Khutlang organisation as a seasonal labour team is a built-in mechanism in agricultural economy both for coordinating the activities of woman individuals, as well as for perpetuating a smooth functioning of the organisation in production.[14]

In a Meitei society, women who are at the ages of forty and sixty appear to have avenues of economic activities. She can be a wholesale trader or work as a broker between the outside agent and the village weavers. She can open a shop or a hotel in the market or in front of her home.

An interesting aspect of the economic system prevalent among the Meitei women is the Marup system, a type of co-operative credit and savings organization. There are different types of Marup called Luhongba Marup, Cheng Marup, Phi Marup or Paisa Marup. The Marup is also an important institution for economic as well as social bonding.

The Marup at Keithel provides an opportunity for making new contacts for women. In Manipur, especially in the valley, the market is run by the women and the transaction of selling and buying is solely done by women.

There are two categories of women in the market. Women become sellers on essential commodities and women as buyers of the same.

In the Khwairamband Market, women who are allotted reserved seats by the Imphal Municipal Council sell a particular commodity. On the other handthere are women who are not allotted seats but who sell their commodities to the women of the first category. The selling and buying of the commodity is usually done in the early hours of the day.

The participation of Meitei women in different socio-economic activities and their roles and responsibilities towards the family members as girl-child, adult, sister, daughter, wife and mother are clearly demarcated. They are duly confined within the four walls and enjoy an enviable freedom of movement in a patrilineal society in contrast to the restricted movements on woman elsewhere.[15]

Mrs. Grimwood rightly remarked that "The Manipuris do not shut up their woman as is the custom in most part of India, and they are much enlightened and intelligent in consequences".[16] R. Brown also remarked that it would be difficult to find a more industrious woman in India than the Manipuris.[17]

There are also other women whose business is to sell eatable things like meals, tea, pakoura, etc to the women vendors and other women coming to the market. There are also some women who give loans to other women in the market and earn daily interest and thereby add to their family income.[18]

Weaving is another source of income for women both in rural and urban areas. The magic of spider's web is said to have inspired weaving in Manipur. Meiteis believe that Leimaren – the goddess of wealth and prosperity entrusted weaving to women to ensure the well being of the society. The use of light shuttle is very important in the history of Manipur. In no time it became the most widely used loom. Meitei women instead of weaving for her family started weaving for the market too. Weaving is a year long pursuit in Manipur. It provides great economic advantages to women. Artistic designs are created and weaving as an art is at its best on such looms. Weaving has reached a high level of accomplishment and its continuation as a profession or a work of art is attributed not only to economic factors alone.

Finer fabrics with new designs are the favourite of the day and the front runner is a woman named Rani. She taught others how to weave. She also buys the finished products of others and sells them in the market.

Chungkham Rani a weaver, designer and entrepreneur lives in Wangkhei. She lost her husband at a tender age of 21 years. Dismissing the advice of remarriages Rani returned to maternal house and instead concentrated on magical colours and skilful designs in clothes she produced on her loom.[19]

She also made silk phi which was called "Engineer Phi". And on these new range of Phi, Rani also revived old and traditional designs like Namthang Khuthat, Luhong Phijin, Ningkham Mayek, Thambal Chepki, Kanap Phibal, Salai Mayek, Lanngam Phi, etc. In her modern design Rani used different types of flowers such as Wakhong, Thambal, Siroi Lily, Takhellei, Leihao, Juba Kusum, Nongyin, etc.

Though Rani's artistic designs and her contribution to the handloom industry are well known, she is yet to get due official recognition at par with her achievement. However, she received certificates of honour for her outstanding contribution and achievement from both the state and the national governments.

In fact, one of the means of Manipur's progress is weaving as it has tremendous export potentials. According to legends "Ima Leimaren" took charge of the market to bring peace and harmony. Women maintain the tradition as they are considered the descendents of 'Ima'.

Handloom products have a wide market not only in Manipur but also outside the state. Traditionally Meitei women weave only for the household. Soon, she realized that weaving could be a reliable source of income. Thus a mutually beneficial relationship began between the vendor and the weaver. The trader provided the weaver with yarn and the weaver in turn brings in her merchandise. However, it is sad to know that the earnings are not commensurate with that of the traders. Entrepreneurs like Bimolata are experimenting with the traditional motives and have found many usages and means to earn more income.

Another designer and entrepreneur is Ng. Bimolata. In her range of marvelously embroidered gossamery innaphi which captures the swan in mid flight and the flowers of heaven among many women of Manipur find their dreams unfolding. And the realization of their dreams is closely interlinked with Bimolata's own dreams. Bimolata opened her shop from the loan she got from Prime Minister Rojgar Yojna (PMRY). The full-fledged production cum-training unit started giving intensive training to educated unemployed girls and women of the society. Bimolata has been instrumental in organizing various fashion shows in the state. She also participated in many exhibitions (Melas) across the country. Not only this she also participated in many entrepreneurship development programmes (EDP) vendor development programmes, etc.

There are many Meitei women who got National Awards in textile designing. Demands for hand woven saris brought in sophisticated looms. Rani-phi and saris from Rani's shop are in great demand. Shops like "Ningthibi Collection" and "Mem's" are exclusively run by women alone. Realising the commercial potentiality, the Ministry of Textiles established a Weavers' Service Centre to impart training and help the weavers in their trade.

Educated Meitei women's role and contributions is immense. There are many educated women working in different government and semi-government services thereby contributing substantial share to the household income.

Apart from these women, there are some women who spend their days toiling hard in the river banks to gather sand and shingles. Their daily earnings range from Rs.60 to Rs.100. With no fixed time for work, these women work as demanded. Working for long hours with lots of physical exertions has taken toll on the health of these women. For these women the sand granules are treasure. With no minimum wage standard, no health care facilities, no insurance for emergencies, they carry on with their work with utmost pride and dedication. May be it is time their needs are taken into consideration and some kind of welfare activities are taken up. Inspite of their labour and contributions in the family maintenance they are not given their due share. Though men and women work equally, women are not given equal wages as male labourers. This shows that Manipuri women are given lower economic position and status in the society inspite of the extent of labour given equally.

(III) MEITEI WOMEN'S ROLE IN POLITICS

In India, the constitution guaranties equality of status to all citizens, which is implicit in the preamble, the fundamental rights and directive principles of state policy. Independent India has accorded equal rights and privileges in all spheres of life, be it social, economic or political.[20] According to Prof. M.C. Arun of Manipur University's Anthropology Department "Our deep rooted hypocrisy toward man and woman in relation to the power equation comes out sharply when a woman is penalized or ostracized for indulging in habits beyond the traditional settings".[21]

Thus, there is no legal obstacle today in the path of the women preventing them from assuming an equal status with men. In Manipur, Meitei women played an important role in shaping the policies and programmes of the state in their individuals and collective capacities. Right from the reign of Pakhangba in 33 AD women actively participated in the administration and state policies as can be seen when Queen Laisana, wife of Pakhangba became the head of the 'Kuchu', an administrative body, along with nine other women. They were known as Laishram Pham. The Kuchu was again divided into two i.e. Lakhong and Laton. The members of Lakhong were the mothers of the King and the Queen and other older women. Other fifteen women known as 'Achoubi' assisted them. Every morning they would discuss the internal matters of the palace. These bodies had the power to judge on the King if he did not follow the rules prescribed by the Lakhong. Laton is also known as 'Leimakhubi Phamlup' which consisted of twelve women members under the leadership of Leimakhubi. Leimakhubi Phamlup discussed the matters of the palace and the state. It is concerned with finance, food-grains, cloth, infantry etc. Thus women were involved in the administration of the state.

During this period, there was also a separate court which was known as 'Pacha Loishang' consisting of women only.

Meitei women inherited an established tradition of movement for social justice, administrative oppressions and misrule of the state authority. The history of Manipur reveals a role of the people, their love for independence. During the Seven Years' devastation or Chahi Taret Khuntakpa (1819-1826), Meitei women rendered valuable help to the princes and freedom fighters of Manipur in their struggle to liberate the land from the hands of the Burmese. Meitei women emerged as a strong political force in collective capacity during the British period. The British authorities took up vigorous measure against the villages which took active part in the Anglo-Manipuri War, 1891. From these villages the British had collected a large number of people and used them as workers on the construction of Mao-Manipur Road". The autocratic policy of the British authorities became unbearable for the people of Manipur.[22]

According to Dr. Chandramani Singh, "The Pressure of colonization has left a mark on the courageous Meitei male population. Meitei men in the past were men of courage and men of pride. Since the British came to Manipur, they have lost it. They wanted to work as servants. They have lost their 'national character'. Our women retained their character. They remain independent and confident. Time has not changed this."[23]

In Manipur, large market centres run by women have a history of providing moral consensus on the political problems of the state, because market is an important venue of social and political interaction. "In the years 1939 and 1904, the state witnessed a great mass movement against colonial and feudal authority of the state solely by the women of Manipur. These movements are the turning points in the emergence of a political and national consciousness."[24]

Women voiced their grievances against the oppressive measures of the British with the introduction of the new colonial administrative system in Manipur. Movements were launched against the increase in water tax rate and Lallup system. These movements "greatly help in the growth of the political and national consciousness."[25]

Again in 1938-39 there was a poor harvest in Manipur. It was caused by several factors. Excessive rainfall in 1939 damaged the standing crops and vegetables. There was near famine in the land due to this. Over and above this the British policy of exporting the rice outside Manipur resulted in the scarcity of rice in the market. Another deep rooted cause of the movement was due to the irregularities and malpractices in the administration of the state. Administrative reports of Manipur of December 1939 said that one Aribam Chaobiton Devi from Tera Keithel organized a small group of about five women and tried to stop the bullock carts carrying paddy for the Marwari traders.

In no time all the women of Khwairamband Bazaar dealing in different trades joined the movement and started to demand the export of rice to be stopped and the workings of the rice mills in Manipur. The movement was spontaneous and very little time was taken in building up the movement. From this movement the demand for introduction of democracy emerged for the first time in Manipur. It is also a fact that the demand for change is always met with resistance".[26]

This proved that women of Manipur are always ready to take mass political action if any action of the Government affected the interest of the people. Meitei women are always alert in protecting the social and political rights of the people. The women of Manipur enjoyed universal adult franchise for the first time in 1948 held under the Manipur State Constitution Act 1947. Women who had attained the age of 21 years exercised their franchise in electing the members of the Manipur State Assembly. It was an important landmark in the political history of Manipur where women were granted adult franchise without any struggle.

Since 1952, Manipuri women have been participating in the political process of the state as voters in every elections. In the parliamentary and Electoral college elections in 1952, Ishwari Devi, wife of late Maharaja Bodhchandra Singh contested election as an independent in the parliamentary constituency. M.K. Binodini contested from Khurai constituency in the Electoral College election as an All Manipur National Union (AMNU) candidate and was elected. But Ishwari Devi was not elected. In the Territorial Council elections in 1957, another women called Smt. Shabi Devi contested as a Communist candidate from Wangkhei Kongba constituency. But she was defeated. There were female members in the Territorial Assembly from 1963-69 by means of nominations. They are Smt. R.K. Mukhra Devi and Smt. A. Bimola Devi and two tribal women were also nominated.

In the Assembly Elections held in 1972, and mid-term elections held in 1974, no women candidate got elected. Only in the year 1992 by-election, Smt. K. Apabi Devi, wife of the sitting MLA K. Bira Singh got elected on Congress ticket after the sudden demise of her husband.

In the Assembly election held in February, 2000, out of the 11 (eleven) women candidates, only Smt. W. Leima Devi got elected.

In the 8th Assembly election, 2002, out of the seven women candidates, only Smt. W. Leima Devi won the election.

In the 9th Assembly election 2007(Mid Term), Smt. Okram Landhoni Devi, wife of Shri O. Ibobi Singh, the Hon'ble Chief Minister of Manipur, was elected from the Khangabok Assembly Constituency.

In Manipur, women could hardly get elected in the Parliamentary elections to join the higher political decision making body.

In the local bodies like Municipalities and Panchayats, after the 73rd and 74th Constitutional Amendment Act of 1992 and 1993, 33% of the total seats were reserved for women. Even in the Zila Parishad and Gram Panchayat elections, women were elected as Pradhans and Gram Panchayat members on the basis of reservations.

Inspite of their involvement and the Panchayati Raj system, women are not free from the power of men from influencing their decisions and actions. Sometimes, these elected women were not capable of addressing the gender issues because most of them were not educated and lacked awareness of the importance of women's participation in the decision making process.

The political role of Meitei women, by and large, is passive but they are socially active. This is partially due to the behavioural constraints the women suffer from. Moreover the society at large is still conservative and clings steadfastly to the traditional role of women as home makers.[27] Women are involved in the women's wings of the various political parties but they have not emerged as leaders at party level.

In order to initiate a breakthrough and to accelerate development with gender equity, social networks of women should be strengthened and women's participation in the decision making should be enhanced. Family members also should co-operate by sharing family responsibilities.

(IV) RELIGIOUS ROLE OF MEITEI WOMEN

Religion has been a constant function in the growth of human civilization. It is readily accepted that "all know-societies have been to some degree religions"[28] It has also been stated that ... given the biological and social nature of man on this planet, some kind of religious system is a cultural universal: no human society can get along without a religion any more than it can survive without an economic system. The actual cultural content found in the religions of different societies may vary enormously, but underlying this diversity there may be impressive similarities in basic functions, involving the culturally prescribed solutions of human social and psychological problems and the way of expressing and re-affirming the central values of a society. Viewed in this light, religion appears to be and essential ingredient of society.[29]

Historically, the religion of the Meiteis can be broadly divided into two namely (i) Traditional religion or Pre-Hindu religion of Manipur, and (ii) the advent and rise of Hinduism in Manipur. R.K. Jhaljit is of the view that the Meiteis worshipped natural objects like Fire, the Sun, Soraren (the God of rain and thunders), the God of the homestead, Wind etc.[30]

About the traditional Meitei religion J. Shakespear states that "The worship of the Umanglai or forest God and other lesser supernatural beings, such as, Sa-roi-nga-roi, evil spirits which are always on the look-out to injure human beings: The Hellois, beautiful female forms which lure foolish men into waste places and then disappear, leaving their victims bereft of reason and Hingchabis and Witches. Originally, there were only nine of these forest gods and seven goddesses, but these have now increased to 364 and the pundits claim that from their books they can trace the pedigree of every one of these 364 divinities back to one or other of the original nine gods and seven goddesses.[31]

The ideas of Hinduism which began to arrive in Manipur with the immigration of a group of people from North India who are referred as Nongchup Haram or Westerners in the traditional manuscripts came to be known Bamon or Brahmin since the time of Pamheiba or Garibaniwaza.[32]

Cheitharol Kumbaba and Sanamahi Laikan record the destruction by Garibaniwaza of Abodes of nine Umanglais were destroyed.[33]

The king started constructing new shrines for Hindu gods and goddesses of the Ramanandi cult. But, inspite of all out efforts of the King and his guru Shanta Das they could not root out the traditional belief of the Meiteis altogether. After facing strong resistance from the people led by one great Maichou popularly known as Lourembam Khongnang Thaba, King Garibniwaza gave royal permission for the worship of the old faith of the Meiteis.

The rise of Vaishnava form of Hinduism reached its pinnacle during the time of King Jai Singh or Bhagyachandra (1763 – 1798 AD). Jai Singh spared no pains to bring about spiritual and material regeneration of his country. His daughters would look after the 'Pujas of Govindaji'. Among the Maha Raj Kumaris, Sija Lairoibi, through her devotion to Govindaji, had high spiritual attainments. Her dance and song reflected her intense devotion. It was 'Lairoibi Sija' the 'Radha of Manipur' who gave concrete shape to an extremely devotional form of dance, conceived by her father Jai Singh. This is the history of the origin of the famous "Rasa dance of Manipur". The princess did not marry. She used to dance before Govindaji, playing the part of 'Rajeswari' she also composed some devotional songs in Bengali to sing for the pleasure of her beloved Lord Govindaji.[34] Sija Lairoibi accompanied her father upto Nabadwip where she spent her days in singing and meditating to Lord Krishna.

Every Meitei home has a tulsi-pung (basil plant on an earthen mound) in the courtyard as a sign of adherence to the

Vaishnava faith. Almost all Meitei women, orthodox men and children who were Vaishnavites wear Chandan marks on their nose and foreheads.[35]

Meiteis women's role in religious life of the society is very unique, especially compared to other Hindu societies in India. The traditional roles of Meitei women are too deep rooted to be subverted by Brahmanic influence. In the Meitei society apart from the Maibis, there are also women who are somewhat religions specialist. They were called Kithumpuba, or Sadhika (holy female). They are self-styled holy people without any formal training or recognition from the Loishang. They can only perform senmit and rites but cannot attend Lai Haraoba festivals. These women wear normal clothes but each of them has personal idiosyncrasies, concerning food colour of dress or some other aspect of lifestyle.

These Sadhika sometimes give prediction and some politicians also go to them for pre-dedication and protection. They were known to have got sudden power and received mantra in a dream or trance.

In fact, while vaishnava culture received major attention from the royal administration, the ancient faith of the Meiteis retained its place in the core religions conceived of the society. Even though sanskritic rituals were introduced into Meitei society these rituals are modified to suit the Meitei ethos. It can be seen in the replacement of Bhratridvitiya (brothers' ritual and feast) with Ningon Chak-Kouba (sister's and daughter's feast) in the mid nineteenth century. This feast or Ningol Chak-kouba strengthened the brother and sister bond of love and also gave security for the sister in a rigidly male dominated society.

Therefore, Meitei religious life is marked by the co-existence of the traditional belief and Vaishnavite Hindu faith.

In religious festivals equal status with men is given to women. In Manipur, women dancing in ceremonies are regarded as 'thougal' (dedication) cuts across all social classes and age groups.

In Meitei society, it is the duty of the women to worship god and goddesses for the welfare and prosperity of the community and the state. Therefore, in every Meitei home the worship of Sanamahi can be found. Hinduism had forbidden women to sing and dance in the ritual arena because the Brahmans regarded them as polluting agents. The present popularity of women Sankirtana can be attributed in part to the courage and seal of a famous female Sankirtana singer called Manimacha Devi. She was the first professional woman to give up the plain looking attire and wear the traditional attire with gold jewelries. She bravely rejected the use of tiny cymbals (manjera) and adopted large khartal (large cymbal) till then used by men. Manimacha Devi formed Sankirtana group of women and started to perform like group of men.

In the midst of such an exuberant Vaishnava environment, the traditional system and belief maintains its strength and character in the Meitei society. Instead of the Brahman priests the Meitei Maibas and especially Maibis play highly important roles in officiating for Meitei Lai worship. Maibis are Manipuri origin and they got assimilated into the social system of the Meiteis. A woman can become a Maibi if she becomes possessed at an early age. But older woman of the age of 50 or 60 can also become a Maibi. Once a woman becomes a Maibi, she does not conform to the standard of Meitei social roles.

The most interesting aspect of a Maibi role is that she holds a special ritual status outside the nonuse of the social frame-work for women. The dress of the Maibi is different from other women of Meitei society. The 'phanek' and 'chaddar' are all white and additional waist wrapper also of white colour is worn on top of the 'phanek'. A long sleeved white blouse is worn and flowers are usually placed in the hair and behind the ears.

"In the contemporary society, the social religious functions of the 'Lai Haraoba' have been greatly affected. During the early and monarchical times its functions was to bring about social solidarity amongst the people of the land; its functions was to serve as a kind of cementing force and establish the control of the monarch over the people through the agency of religious institutions like Pundit Loishang. The Pundit Loishang controlled the performance of the Lai Haraoba festivals by granting permission, sending Maiba, Maibis and pena singers and in some cases sending royal horses, elephants etc for the performance of a Lai Haraoba. However, due to the change in the political and social systems of Manipur, particularly after the abolition of monarchial system and 'merger' of Manipur with the Indian union on 15th October, 1949, the control of Pundit Loishang in the religious matter of the land has been greatly diminished if not lost altogether. Whatever little power and privileges left for the king was also removed in 1972. Under this changed political system, the king of Manipur lost its meaning even in the religious system, and the same was the case with other institutions associated with the monarchial system such as Pundit Loishang. This process of democratization in the body polity and society of Manipur in turn affected the social role of Lai Haraoba, which is, of course, an inseparable part of the traditional religion of Manipur. There has been recently a great increase in the number of traditional deities for which Lai Haraoba is performed. These trends reflect the urge to re-assert the unique cultural identity of the indigenous people of the land".[36]

It is religious belief which empowers these women mystics and through which they can claim moral power in the name of God. And it is this belief that cut across gender divisions as it is by definition shared by men and women. It neither individuated nor apparently emerged from their conviction of a subjection to God and their dedication to a higher cause, which enable them to overcome certain man-made customs and which provides them with a sense of intimacy with the divine. The mysticism of the Maibis allows them freedom to move above and beyond not only from an expected role of a domesticated housewife or a nurturing mother, but also the precondition for access to wisdom of self sufficiency and spiritual growth. The break with domesticity is also in effect a rejection of a primary domain where sexuality is customarily regulated.

The Maibis of Manipur reflect an interchangeable aspect of priesthood and shamanism. They can take on the roles of both priestesses performing religions rites and mystics preoccupied with acts of exorcism and healing or cursing. The old tradition of paying homage to local Meitei lai or gods merged with the other forms of appeasing more popular gods such as, Krishna, Shiva, etc. The invasion of the vaishnavite tradition into the social strata of the Meitei society, could not stop women devotees and women mystics to participate in the religions rites of the Meiteis.

The influx of the Vaishnav tradition of worship resulted simultaneously in the transgression and reformulation of patriarchal ideologies. In the course of time, the Maibis became sometimes the preferred mediums than their male counterparts. The Maibas in some cases for conducting religions affairs in the palace and at other religious places in Manipur.

There is an implicit understanding here that gender is both a social function and an expressive mode, that gender is culturally constructed and so gender function may be interchanged.

The religions fervour of the Maibis and the mystical overtones that surround their very being empowers them and to a large extent enables them to transcend andocentric cultural categories. In Manipur, the Maibis occupy a position that is no less that of a cultural connoisseur. The lethal combination of the Meira Paibis who would agitate against perceived threats to their society and the Maibis who would give them complete spiritual support reflect the peculiar conditions of women's lived experiences within the Manipuri society, ordinarily the shared experiences of a 'subculture' may be marginal to the male public/political world, but that is equally acknowledged and indispensable to the healthy functioning of a balanced society. The energies of the women participants in the various social and religious movements is more than often channeled into strong female bonding networks that cut across caste and class structures.

An exploration of the tradition of the Maibis not only tells one about certain social value and pressure operating in the Manipuri society but also offers a glimpse into the symbolic universe of the local culture in which its various traditions are embedded.

Thus, Meitei women's role in religion is something unique. Unlike other parts of India, there is no restriction for women to participate in the religious Kirtans or festivals observed in the temples. Women are allowed to sing in the Shradha ceremony as well as in weddings. Inspite of being patriarchal society Meitei women participated actively in every religious festival observed in the society.

References

1. Mrs. Grimwood, My Three Years in Manipur; Cultural Publishing House, Delhi, 1975; pp. 58-59.

2. Dun E.W., Gazetteer of Manipur; Vivek Publishing House, Delhi, 1957, p. 17.
3. Dr. M.C. Arun; Anthropology Department, M.U. A two-day seminar on "The Social Status on Women of North East India", 3-4 June, 2005 at Senate Hall, M.U., Imphal.
4. O. Bhogeswor Singh (ed), Ningthourol Lambuba, Imphal, 1967; p. 92.
5. Ibid; pp..310-311.
6. N. Khelchandra (ed), Chada Laihui; Imphal, 1966; pp.63-66.
7. Prof. Ksh. Bimola Devi, The Changing Role of Manipuri Women; p. 30.
8. Nandalal Sharma, Meitrabak, O.K. Store, Imphal, 1960; pp.72-73.
9. Raghumani Mangang, Meitei Laws and Usages, Lanmei Thanbi Publishing Association, Imphal; 1988; p. 66.
10. History of Manipur (1826-1949), Edited by Dr. Lal Dena, 1991; pp. 95-96; Orbit Publishers & Distributors; New Delhi.
11. Manjushree Chaki Sirkar, Feminism in a traditional Society, Shakti Book House, Delhi, 1984; p. 10.
12. O. Bhogendro Singh,Op. Cit, 1967; p. 524.
13. B. Kulachandra Singh, The High Status That the Law of Manipur Accorded to Meitei Women, Manipur Text, Macha Leima, No.15, Dec. 2001; p. 5.
14. Mani Babu, M. (1990) 'Meetei Women's' working team in Agriculture : A non-nuclear approach on an organisation in production – Anthropology Department (Dibrugarh University, Assam).
15. Goswami M.C. & C.B. Singh; Patron and Patroness-client; Relations in Thanga marketing organisation; Bulletin of the Anthropology Department, Gauhati University, 1972; pp. 45-57.
16. Grimwood, E. St. C. My Three Years in Manipur, Delhi : Vivek Publishing House, 1975; pp. 58-59.
17. Brown. R; Statistical Account of Manipur, 1873, Calcutta; p.76.

18. Ksh. Bimola, "Manipur Women in the Present Day Society – An observation" Women, Vol. II, MUWWA, Imphal, 1996; p. 11.
19. Interview with Rani Chungkham, 15 April, 2006, Wangkhei, Imphal.
20. D.D. Basu, Introduction to the Constitution of India, New Delhi, 1983.
21. Prof. M.C. Arun, In Imphal Free Press, dated December, 9, 2007.
22. N. Khelchandra (ed) Cheitharol Kumbaba Manipur Sahitya Parishad, Imphal; p. 497.
23. Personal interview : Dr. Chandramani Singh, November 9, 2007.
24. Nupi Lan- Edited by Longjam Meitei Netaji (Tera Keithel), 1980.
25. Singh. W. Joykumar, Social Movements in Manipur (1917-1951); Mittal Publication, New Delhi, 1992.
26. N. Joykumar, Social Movements in Manipur, Mittal Publications, New Delhi, 1992; p..1.
27. Interview : Dr.(Mrs.) Ch. Jamini Devi, Chairman, Manipur State Commission for Women on 17th Oct., 2007.
28. Betty R. Schart : The Sociological study of Religion; p. 30.
29. William A. Lessa and Evon Z. Vogt : Reader in Comparative Religion (4th Edn); p. 36.
30. R.K. Jhaljit : A Short History of Manipur; p. 26.
31. J. Shakespear,: The Religion of Manipur : Folklore Transactions of the folklore society, Vol. XXIV, No. IV; Dec 1913; p. 421.
32. Y. Munan Meitei : Bamon Khunthoklon; p. 3.
33. Cheitharol Kumbaba; p. 87.
34. J. Roy : History of Manipur; p. 53.
35. Manjusri Chaki-Sircar : Feminism in A Traditional Society (Women of the Manipur Valley), Vikas Publishing House Pvt. Ltd.; p. 102.

36. Dr. Khumanjao Ratan Kumar – Lai Haraoba of Manipur (Indigenous festival of the Meiteis – A Socio-Historical perspective); pp. 131-132.

3

Role of Meitei-Pangal Women

(I) ROLE OF MEITEI-PANGAL WOMEN IN SOCIETY

The Muslims of Manipur locally known as “Pangals” are part of Manipuri society. The influence of Meitei culture is so great that, the Meitei culture and Islamic ideology are complimentary to each other in mounding the essence of “Pangal society”. The only differences in these two societies is religion. The influence of Meitei culture over the Muslims in Manipur is so great that perhaps that is one of the reason why they are called “Meitei Pangal”.

Col. McCulloch wrote “the Munniporee Mussalman population arose from Munniporee men having taken as wives Mussalman women ... before the regular introduction of Hindooism”.[1]

T.C. Hudson remarked ‘the Muhammadans were distinct from the Meitei’ and a special panchayat court sits at Lilong, for the trial of cases between Muhammadan Manipuris.[2]

It has been generally accepted that the Muslims of Manipur first settled in Manipur after King Khagemba captured them in a war, in 1606. L. Iboongohal Singh fixed the year in 1605 AD. According to "Cheitharol Kumbaba" the incident was occurred in 1528 Saka era. "The King of Manipur gave them Manipuri girls as their wives. They numbered about one thousand".[3]

Mirza Fazlul Quadir, however, wrote that Manipur Muslims grew out of the local converts into Islam. He wrote "very few Muslims from the rest of India went and settled in Manipur state. The major portion of Manipur's Muslim population is by conversion. Muslims never ruled in that territory. During British rule, only few Muslims from other parts of India settled in Manipur state".[4]

Manipur has been a home to several ethnic communities. The valley of Manipur has now assumed a cosmopolitan character, although the Meitei Hindus and Muslims are numerically preponderant. Muslims constitute 6.9% of the total population as per 2001 census and are spread in the four valley districts. Around 70% of the population resides in the rural areas.[5]

The London School of Oriental and African Studies made available a document in 1983 (also translated in the 'preface' of the Pangal Thorakpa Puya by R.K. Sanahal Singh, 1985/89, VII-XI) which made studies on the process of the formation of various clans about 50 in number. The document noted that the palace Pandits (Meitei Scholars) are of the view that Manipuri Muslim clan formation initiated with what is named as the 'Aribam Sagei since the period of King Nouphangba (590-680 AD). This Pangal population found in 930 A.D. was adept in preparing salt from dug wells, since their Muslim coreligionists used to collect salt from the Bengal Sea according to B. Kulachandra Sharma (1997:62). Ningthourol Lambuba described the two Pasha and one Pangal-village flourished during the reign of King Irengba (984-1074 AD) (O. Bhogeshwor; 1967 : 74, 94). Living at Khuga Valley at that time, these pangals introduced the practice of 'Rice broadcast and transplantation' procedure in Manipur....... The fact that Muslims settled in Manipur, learnt the local language, lived in harmony with the local people, accepted local wives, adopted various professions suited to their genius and that in their dietary system and dwelling houses they depended on materials locally available, bear out that they considered Manipur as their homeland.[6]

Many Manipuri Historians believe that the Muslims, who settled in Manipur came from the west and such Muslims are locally known as Meitei Pangals or Manipuri Muslims.[7]

Some historians gave the time of their arrival and settlement in Manipur was the time of King Mungyamba (1562 – 1597 AD) King Khagemba (1597 – 1652 AD) and their successors.

In the history of the Manipuri Muslims written in 'Urdu'[8], mention may be made about Aribam Sagei also. It is stated that during the reign of King Mungyamba, three Muslims named Seikh Rula, Gora Khan and Ashiq Shah came to Manipur Rajabari (Probably Khaspur) and they settled in Manipur with the royal permission and manufactured muskets for the King.

These three Muslims married Manipuri women and they were the forefathers of one Manipuri Muslim clan known as Aribam Sagei, which is the oldest clan. The sons of these Muslims served as Soldiers under King Khagemba and they played an important role in defeating Sanongba in his first rebellion against his brother Khagemba.[9]

The battle fought between the two brothers was a turning point in the history of Manipur. Khagemba, who won the battle, took the followers of Sanongba as prisoners of war. Those Muslims were given Manipuri women as their wives and allowed them to settle in Manipur with their families. Their settlement in Manipur was the main factor of the foundation of Meitei Pangal (Manipuri Muslim) community in Manipur from the ethnic point of view, they are akin to the Meiteis with whom they share common language known as Meiteilon and the essentials of social structure.

As such 'Meitei Pangals' may be termed as the 'Second Meiteis' of Manipur, who profess Islam as their religion.

The Muslims who settled in Manipur were mostly soldiers and artisans etc. They were deeply engaged in Manipuri army, cultivation, religion, culture and family life etc. It may, therefore, be said that Muslim elements played a distinctive role in the social life of Manipur at various times. From the time of their settlement in Manipur the Muslims had their own Qazis (Magistrate) to administer their personal laws.

Janab Khan also called the Pangals as 'Manipuri Muslims'[10] and R. Brown first used the word 'Meitei Pangal'.[11]

According to Constantine R., "Hindu and Muslim relation in Manipur are a lodestar for the rest of India. The Muslims in the land came from outside, found wives among the local womenfolk and settled down. The Maharaja did not treat them as aliens".[12]

Muslim societies like many other societies harbor illusions about immutable gender differences. Islam is neither more nor less patriarchal than any major religions, especially Hinduism and the other two Abrahamic religions, Judaism and Christianity, all of which share the view of woman as wife and mother. The very fact that, the very mention of Muslim women brings to the minds of many, a vision of veiled maids in dark rooms, illiterate and subdued.

But in reality Islam gives high respect, rights and status to women. Islam presents the roles of men and women as complimentary roles and not contradictory or conflicting ones. In Manipur, Pangal women inhabit in all the four valley districts of Manipur sharing the same environment with women of the Meitei community.

The Meitei Pangals are all orthodox Sunni Muslim, following Islam not only as religion but also as a way of life. Being influenced by the Meitei culture the Manipur Muslim women have more affinity with the Meitei women than other Muslim women outside Manipur.

Therefore, one can assume that the Meitei Pangals occupy a unique and distinctive place in the history of Manipuri society.

The life style of Manipur Muslim women is basically family centered and they have a strong sense of community. But they did not define themselves primarily in terms of their differences from other groups as well. In Manipur Muslim families play a distinctive role on the life style of their womenfolk.

It was the compulsion of modern day governance and administration that necessitated the confining of people as part of one group or the other, thereby disregarding the overlapping boundaries that existed thus far. People were fitted in categories that the colonial authorities fashioned for them.

In Manipur the social structure of the pangals is patriarchal. The women's role was confined within the four walls of the house, women's social positions are quite varied and within the same Muslim society, social class largely determines the degree of sex segregation, female autonomy and mobility. Today in Manipur, and all the Muslim nations upper class women have more mobility than lower class women, although in the past it was the reverse; veiling and seclusion were upper class phenomena. By examining changes over time and variations within societies and by comparing Muslim and non Muslim gender patterns, one recognizes that the status of women in Muslim societies is neither uniform nor unchanging nor unique, except among Manipuri pangals.

Jaunty structure of the Manipur Muslim society is extended, patriarchal and occasionally polygamous. The concept of sanctity and privacy of family life remains strong and a high premium is placed on the good sexual conduct of its female members. In the past such conduct was guaranteed via segregation of women in the 'forbidden' sectors of the house – the hareem or harem. Although harems are not followed in Manipur among the Meitei Pangal women are still more closely associated with the domestic chores and living arrangements of the household.

In rural areas especially the Meitei Pangals treat their women as lower beings. The life style of the women in the Meitei Pangal society is simple. They have a strong sense of community.

The social structure of the pangals being patriarchal, the first and foremost duty of a pangal wife is to serve her husband and to satisfy him morally and physically. She works for the family by cooking, washing, gardening, watering the plants, rearing domestic animals etc. It is also her duty to teach her children Islamic etiquettes to be maintained in respect of food, dress, manners and other habits which are not compatible with Islamic morality.

The Muslims have a number of customs and prohibitions e.g. taboo on eating pork, strict prohibition of portrayals of God as well as any living creature, person, or animal, in worshipping and prohibition in drinking wine. Tokarev, however, wrote that the ban in drinking is not observed everywhere.[13]

According to several authentic hadiths including the one narrated in Ahmed Ibn-e Majah "paradise lies at the feet of the mother". Therefore, a Muslim wife and mother have the right to get good treatment and care from her children. Practically, in a good family, the role of a mother is greater than that of the father. It is here young girls learnt from home the Holy Quran, the Hadiths and Islamic traditions.

Education was deemed not necessary for the women except for theological lessons. For the Muslims education has always been transmitted through traditional schools called Maktabs, Madrasas and Khanqah. While the problems and constraints of education and employment of the youth in the Muslim community received great attention, the education of women was not an issue at all. Rather education of males in the community was considered as pre-requisite for female education even in Manipur. It was the male mindset of the Meitei Pangal community who enforced these practices and it was thought that unless they were educated there was no hope that women will have access to educational opportunities. Due to the strict seclusion of women in the society women education became an obstacle the instruction of girls at beyond a very elementary level.[14]

For the Muslim, education means a girl has to know how to recite the Holy Quran, how to be a devoted wife, an excellent future mother with expertise in household work and above all punctuality in the religious duties.

In Manipur, the Manipuri Muslim women's status in education has not improved in any significant way. The reason for this could be lack of interest resources, discrimination in accessing resources and opportunities. Thus, while Muslims are culturally close to other religions and ethnic communities in India, there are significant differences in social and material conditions of Meitei Muslim as compared to other religions group, which places them in a position of relative disadvantage. As there is no Middle High Schools in the Muslim concentrated areas there was greater number of dropouts of girls than boys. In rural areas it is almost nil as there were no schools nearby their localities.

It is by sheer determination that Muslim girls studied upto Master degree level. According to the report of the socio-economic survey of Meitei Pangal 2004 brought out by Directorate of Economic and Statistics and Directorate of Minorities and Other Backward Classes give a rate of 40 per cent. Among the Muslims, Meitei pangal women unfortunately, seemed unable to adapt themselves to time suited or issue related information as to what is happening elsewhere especially in the state capital i.e. Imphal. Meitei Muslim women like any women of other societies have to face the same problems like bringing up children, to bring them up according to the strict norms of Islamic culture and also face the problems of in-laws as daughter in-laws.

Now-a-days modern education has taught Meitei Muslim women to be aware of the developments among them and they have the ability, knowledge and capacity to face the problems of everyday life. They now have the right to freedom of worship and the freedom to move or follow any occupation inspite certain restrictions, duties and obligation.[15]

Muslims have a number of customs – and marriage is considered the sole legitimate way of carnal satisfaction. Hughes contended that "The celebration of the marriage is called Nikaah .... Marriage is enjoined upon every Muslim"[16]

Marriage among the Muslims is "a civil contract and like contracts, it cannot be validated under duress. Essentially it is a relation of love based on the spouse's willingness to have the union and it is supposed to strengthen faith and to further the cause of Islam".[17]

According to Islamic laws a man can marry any girl or woman except (1) his mother; (2) his mother's sisters; (3) his father's sister; (4) his sisters; (5) Step-mother and her daughters; (6) his daughters; (7) his brother's daughters; (8) his sister's daughters; (9) his sons' wife or wives; (10) his wife's daughters (who are born to other husbands); (11) his wife's sister; (12) his foster mother; and (13) other women who are nursed by his foster mother."[18] Marriage with these women are prohibited.

Though one can marry any woman except taboo ones, the pangals do not generally marry close relatives or with clan members. The pangals believed that marriage between clan members result in the birth of defective or deformed children. This practice seems to be adopted from the Meiteis, who adopted the system of exogamy. Performance of Nikah is the most important characteristic of marriage for the Muslim community in Manipur. In some families Nikah is performed on the day of marriage while in some families marriages are performed after some months of Nikah. 'Mehr' is the bride price to be paid by the groom. It is not a fixed one in Manipur but decided by the status and capability of the groom.

In a Meitei Pangal society widows, widower and divorcees are allowed to remarry. But all marriages of the widows should be performed from their parental houses but not from the houses of the in-laws. It is believed that "a Muslim woman is obedient to her husband not because of any inferiority but because she accepts him as her guardian".[19]

In a pangal society, widows, widowers and divorcees are allowed to remarry. Islamic law also recognises the right of both parties to dissolve the marriage under certain given circumstances. Islam discourages divorce in principle but permits it only when it has become altogether impossible for the parties to live together in peace and harmony.

But in Manipur among the Meitei Pangals "divorcees forced their ex-wives to resume marriage (which is forbidden) without having been married to another man. Therefore, they used to hire a man to marry momentarily the ex-wife and divorce them after a few days of marital life". Such unnatural marriages are called "Nikah khutnek" (Hired wedlock by the pangals)".[20]

In Manipur, females could seek divorce under some conditions. The most prevalent system is done by writing a document called "Kabi Nama" in which some conditions are imposed on the husband, failing which the marriage becomes null and void. This is done in order to check the high handed authority of the husband. It may be noted that with the coming of modernity in the Pangal society many changes can be seen in the society. Girls have the right to choose their husband now. According to Mrs. Aman from Keibung Thawan in her days parents arranged the marriage of their daughters and there is a saying in Meiteilon that, "Phanek Phiban Tatlaga Mou Phang-i" [21] which shows much labour is required in order to get a wife or (a mou). Pangal society is undergoing gradual changes and Meitei Pangal women are now aware of their rights and liberty.

The Meitei Pangals used to invite their relatives and members of their Shagei in any customary function and ritual. The customary function performed prior to the marriage ceremony is known as "Sagei Kwa Yenba, Kwa Khaib and Panuka Puba.

Sagei Kwa Yenba :- After giving the hand of the daughter in marriage, the Sagei Kwa Yenba is performed. The father of the boy engages a person for this purpose and sends him along with betel nuts and leaves for distribution to the 'sagei' (relative) of the girl.

Kwa Khaiba :- After the sagei kwa yenba the Kwa Khaiba (cutting of betel nuts into four square pieces) function is performed on a date agreed to between the parents of the boy and the girl. After the invitees assemble one or two of the old ladies present remove the skin of green betel nuts and cut them into four equal pieces. If the pieces of nuts are found without any defect, it is considered a good omen. The betel nuts with leaves along with sweets brought by the boy's side are distributed to all the people who assemble for the ceremony. This function is performed for formal declaration of the agreement between boy's and girls' parents for the marriage of their children.

Panuka Puba :- The panuka is a compound word of Pan and Kwa (betel leaves and nuts). This system is a counterpart of the Heijing Pot puba of the Meiteis. Friends of the girl to be married and relatives of both the girl and boy are invited. Betel leaves and nuts are arranged in pieces in a packet called putla. Sweet meats and fruits are also included. These are distributed to the guests but a special share of the items is reserved for the girl and her friends.

Again under the influence of the Mapam Chakkouba of the Meitei marriage 'Hiram' is becoming a very important part of the marriage ceremony of the Meitei Muslims in Manipur. Heavy dowry is not compulsory, but apart from giving dowry in kind or in cash, it is compulsory to give a copy of the Quran by the father to his daughter on the marriage day.

Meitei Muslim women speak Meiteilon though most of them can speak Arabic.[22] They also use Meitei phanek in their daily lives including Meitei phanek Mayek Naiba in some social functions. Among Meitei Pangal women, the condition of their health is low when compared with other communities of the state. Most of the Meitei Muslims belief in Maibas for treatment of their ailments rather than professional doctors.

The Meitei pangal women lack health consciousness and due to lack of exposure and restrictions imposed on women they lack awareness and skill. Perhaps this is due to lack of education among the women folk. But in this present scenario, Meitei pangals except in remote areas started sending their daughters to schools and colleges in urban areas. Because, they now realized that working women in every field perform their duties well. No women working as government employee can be found in any department. There are some women who observe purdah in their work places.

In rural areas girls go to the market before going to school to sell their vegetables. Thus, in this way girls also help their parents to enhance their meager earning. The pangal society has started religious schools or Madrasa for women under the scheme of Sarva Shiksha Aviyan. Schemes like the Prime Minister's 15 point programme and formal and Adult Education and also scheme of Mid Day Meal are not implemented satisfactorily in Muslim concentrated areas in rural sector.23

But schools for women was established at Kairang Heikru Makhong (Ipum Khongban) and in Irong Mayai Leikai, etc. Unfortunately, most of the women in pangal society are not aware of things around them.

They should be given proper education only then could they be made aware of opportunities and rights which are theirs for the taking. This would greatly improve the society and also raise the status of Meitei pangal women in Manipur.

(II) ROLE OF MEITEI PANGAL WOMEN IN POLITICS

In Islam, a woman has the right to involve in political activities and it also believed that a woman can influence political scenes. In Islam women are given the right to approach directly the head of the community to redress their grievances and they have the voting right too. When Hazrat Ali (RA) was appointed Caliph, people sought the approval of the Prophet Muhammad's (pbuh) wife Bibi Ayesha. According to some Hadiths, it is undesirable for a woman to be a leader of a nation, but it cannot be termed as Haram (unlawful). If necessary, a woman can become the leader of a State. If one looks at the Holy Quran, Sura Alag, Ayat No.1-5 and 28-35 the act of teaching and learning has been accorded a lot of importance. In Sura Baqr, Prophet of Islam has himself said, "Learning is a must for every Muslim man and woman." (Ibu Majid) Muslim women are often illiterate or half illiterate which is very disheartening inspite of Islam's encouragement of learning for women.

We have seen that Islam came to India almost immediately after the death of the Holy prophet and some maintain that Islam came during the life time of the prophet. From the time of their earliest settlement, women played a significant historical role. For example, Raziya's mother was the most prominent among Iltutmish's queen. Qazi Minhaj was deeply impressed by her munificence to the Ulemas, holy men, Sayyids and Muslim ascetics. Raziya herself not only commanded the army against rebel Igtadars but she was also a brilliant administrator. Emperor Babur's wife Maham Begum participated in state matters sitting beside the emperor on the throne. Makan Hamida Banu, wife of Emperor Humayun was a capable advisor. King Shah Jahan's wife Mumtaz Mahal was the emperor's leading advisor and councilor and after her death her place was taken by her daughter Jahan Ara. She exercised power in the administration.

Father Monserrate reported that "the Imperial farmans (royal decrees) were sealed eight days after they were received from the Wazir by one of the queens in whose keeping is the royal signet ring and also the seal of the realm."[24] During Shah Jahan's reign the small signet (Uzuk) was kept in Mamtaz Mahal's custody. On the queen's request it was handed over for some years to her father, Asaf Khan (the Wakil). After Mumtaz Mahal's death it was controlled by her daughter, Jahan Ara.[25] Therefore, this shows that women of early Islamic days present a sharp contrast to the disempowered Indian Muslim women of today. Religious studies, medicine, trade, teaching, social service and nursing were the fields where women created history during that time. Hazrat Khatija (R.A.A.) was a business woman and the services of Mohammad (SAW) were hired by her.

Hazrat Ayesha another wife of the prophet "knows more about the injunctions of Holy Quran, Poetry and literature, the history of the Arabs and their hierarchy than any other person".[26] She had knowledge about medicine, accounts and legal matters as well. Besides, the wives of the nobles used to accompany as nurses in battlefields where they used to work as suppliers and controllers of essential commodities. When we compare the situation with the contemporary life style of Indian Muslim women, especially Muslim women in Manipur we find a lot of differences.

Inspite of being marginalized, segregated and disempowered economically and politically, women in Pangal society are courageous and active. It is true that women in early Islamic days issued religious fatwas (verdict). Some women, who have left a mark are Hazrat Ayesha, Hazrat Fatima Bin Qaib, Hazrat Jaiwara, etc.

In Manipur, Meitei Pangal women, for the development of their society formed many organisations at the local level as well as the state level. Some of them are the Kanglei Muslim Chanura Development Organisation (KMCDO) with its headquarters at Hatta, Imphal East is the biggest Muslim organization in Manipur. Many Muslim local organizations and Meira Paibis among the Meitei Pangal women participated in the peace rally organized by Apunba Manipur Kanba Lup (AMKIL), All Manipur Club Organisation (AMUCO) and the National Identity Protection Committee (NIPCO) on the 20th September, 2000.

The women of Pangal society also took part in the sit-in-protest organized in different places of Manipur against the demand for creation of a greater Nagaland by the National Socialist Council of Nagaland (NSCN). They also took part in the movements organized against illegal activities of the security personnel of the Indian Army or State army when they resorted to tortures, unwarranted arrests or alleged rape.

Meitei Pangal women also supported the movements of the All Manipur Anti Drug Association (AMADA) and the Committee on Anti Drug and alcohol (CADA). According Dr. Th. Binarani, these Muslim organizations are working as a pressure group for safeguarding women's right and for the development of the society as a whole. The Ushoipokpi Tharourok Women Development Association, Ushoipokpi, Lilong is another such organization which was established in the year 2000.

In modern politics, Meitei-pangal women are given by the community only voting rights but they are not allowed to take part in the decision making body. The 73rd Amendment Act of 1992 of the Indian Constitution gave 1/3rd women reservation system in the three tier system of local self government. There are many Meitei Pangal women in Zilla Parishads, Councillors, Pradhans and Members in different tier of local self government. These women work actively in their concerned political areas inspite of their lack of educational qualifications. These women are not simply acting out roles prescribed for them by religion, by culture or by neo-patriarchal states. They are questioning their roles and status demanding social and political change. Participating in movements and taking sides in ideological battles. In particular, they are the centre of the new social movements for democratization, civil society and citizenship.

It should be noted that even the Meiteis who are Hindus and Meitei Pangal who are Muslims, though followed different religions, their economic and political interests are always the same. Culturally and socially they have developed common ways of life.

The political background of Meitei Pangal women and the Muslim Community in general since early 20th century has shaped their present marginal socio-economic legal and political existence. Their political presentation has been negligible which over a period of time has resulted in them being deprived of the benefits of development processes. The Meitei Pangal society must start working on self help basis. It is obvious that religions, political social and economic forces are not supporting their development. Quality education and vocational/ professional training for women will definitely assist the whole community in getting proper share in the fruits of political development as we know that only those who get rewarded who strive for it.[27]

Political conflict or ethnic conflict can bring social change, including change in economic and political status of women, a heightened sense of gender awareness and political activism on the part of women.

Voluntary action is the most important measure to improve the contemporary ethos. Efforts should begin with awareness generation and social education. Slowly and gradually vision of the whole community should be changed. Political rights, the right to contest the larger decision making bodies must be given to the Meitei Pangal women. They should be given the space to participate in the political process and decision making body. This will be possible only when the women are given proper education and freedom from the chain of social bindings and traditions.

(III) ROLE OF MEITEI PANGAL WOMEN IN ECONOMY

Woman is considered a home maker in Islam and not a housewife because she is not married to a house. She can also work and she is entitled to get equal remuneration if she is doing the same job as that of the male. There is no text in the holy Quran which makes it unlawful for women to work or do any lawful job or profession provided it is within the modesty level and is within the purview of the Shariah. Women have no financial obligations in Islam. It is the duty of the men to look after the financial aspect of the family. Therefore, under normal conditions a woman need not work and is not required to earn her livelihood or that of her family. However, in certain genuine cases due to financial crisis in the family where both ends do not meet, she has the option to work with the permission of her husband. Islamic law gives more financial security to women than to men.

The Pangals of Manipur occupy a unique and distinctive place in the society. They were not strict followers of Islam at first. "The Mohammedans of this country are very ignorant of their religion".[28]

The economic conditions of the Meitei Pangal during the years following their initial settlement in Manipur was believed to be good.

In the year 2001 population census, the percentage share of the Muslim workers to the total state workers was found to be 7.42% only. Further, the number of Muslim workers to the total Muslim population was recorded at 36.75%, while out of the total population of Manipur, the percentage of workers was 43.62% at the state level. According to the Socio-Economic Survey of the Meitei Pangal, 2004, 71.17% of the total population is found to be out of the labour force, while 28.83% are in the labour force, of which 24.14% are employed and 4.69% are unemployed.[29]

The Socio-Economic setting of the Muslims in the state is strikingly rural-based, who still subsist on the age old agro oriented pursuits. Agriculture is the mainstay of almost 80% of the Muslims in the state. Merely 2.27 percent of the Muslims are in the Government sector, while the remaining population is engaged in various categories of low-profile, informal or unorganized economic activities like hotel industry, rickshaw pulling, repairing and assembling of cycles, tricycles and motor vehicles etc.[30]

Therefore, it is the women who play a great role in the society. Agriculture being the main occupation of the state, it is the women who go to the fields and work from morning till evening. Muslim women also take up work in handloom weaving, embroidery, poultry farming, etc. In the rural areas, the Muslim women perform excellent work in gardening also. They can sell their local produces to a nearby market throughout the year. They also rear chickens, ducklings, etc for commercial purposes. There is a saying among the Meiteis that a Muslim couple can send their son to study post graduation degree outside with the help of a hen.

While the husband is the bread earner, the wife is the best housekeeper. However, it is also her duty to contribute some help to her husband for the sake of establishing an economically independent family by doing some domestic works of economic importance. In respect of vegetable cultivation it is the women who take the lead for producing marketable vegetables such as cabbage, mustard leaves, radish, carrots, palaks, onion, chilly etc. Almost all the activities such as vegetable cultivation, weaving and arrangement for disposal of the marketable goods at the terminal markets or direct to the capital market in Imphal are carried out by the womenfolk. The life style of the Muslim women are home centred which is suitable for them under the purdah system and other conditions of the Islamic systems. There are also some salary earning Muslim women in Manipur. The share of Muslim women in white coelared jobs are very low and less than one per cent of the total Muslim population in the state. This handful of salary earners are found only in urban areas.[31] Muslim women in general rely as a source income by venturing into vegetable markets and vendors at roadside of public places and very few could make their way to Khwairamband Bazar. Many of them work as domestic helpers and also work as door to door peddlers.

In urban areas, women are also found working in small bakeries, hotels, small scale factories as labourers. Muslim women, it appears, have no recourse to legal remedy for their grievances in the society.

Women's business activities are hampered by the fact that they are largely rural based, and produce from kitchen gardens is only enough for the family, and for sale in adjoining villages. Poor infrastructure and communication system, and a late start in education are causes of backwardness in Manipuri Muslims. There are only a few wealthy households among the Meitei Pangal Community.[32]

The highest annual income earning source is wages and salaries, followed by enterprises and then loans. On the expenditure side, the highest monthly disbursement per household is spent on construction of assets and the least on gifts and charities with the higher percentage of households in the lower income range, it is likely that most of the income is spent on consumption, leaving little for saving and investment.[33]

The community leadership only too immersed in maintaining and strengthening their patriarchal stronghold can hardly do anything to uplift the status of the women. At the same time, by making women the primary workers of their communal identity, they are using their shoulders to place the gun to fire at the "enemy". The State by recognizing only the conservative elements of the community as leaders is deliberately glossing over the injustice faced by women in the name of "respecting minority culture" and identity. The voices from the progressive secular and intellectual sections of the community are too weak and fragmented to have any impact. The women's movement for a long time has worked on the premise that women have a separate existence apart from their community identity. Having realized that this is not so, they have a long way to go in mobilizing Muslim women around their rights.[34]

Miniature versions of the Khwairamband Bazar of Imphal can be seen in almost all the Muslim settlement areas. One of the biggest can be seen at Lilong, the highest Muslim concentration area, almost 6 km from Imphal city. These local markets play an important role in rural development. Besides providing service and outlets for rural produce, these markets ensure the efficiency of food distribution system and inter community linkages.[35]

Women are perceived as wives and mothers and gender segregation is customary and legally required. Whereas economic provision is the responsibility of the men, women must marry, reproduce to earn status. A woman can work and travel only with the written permission of her male guardian. Family honour and good reputation, or the negative consequences of shame, rest most heavily upon the conduct of the women. Again in Muslim society gainful employment by women is not perceived as part of their role. Muslim women generally are not encouraged to work outside the household, taking up job or starting a business is not usually appreciated by others in the community. Restriction on their mobility, early marriages and purdah system are other problems which create obstacles in education. The general lower status of women makes their education the last priority in the family. Sometimes the family feels that money should be saved for their dowry. Due to these few reasons and their may be other reasons too, Muslims in general lack education and awareness. Ability is closing so many doors for Muslim women. Things are improving, but improvements are by and large superficial. Moreover, they are limited to urban areas.

Inspite of the rising rate of literacy in Manipur, Muslim women are still way behind in the field of education. There is no significant change in the society. In Manipur, the dropping out percentage of Muslim women is very high comparatively to other communities. Muslim women lack entrepreneurial skill when compared with the Meitei women.

Therefore, the economic condition of the Muslim women is very low and below satisfactory. The Muslim women should be made aware of the importance of education especially in rural areas and they should be made aware of the benefits of various development programmes launched by the state administration. More self-help groups units should be opened and more empowerment should be given to local bodies. This will help the women to come out to the public fields and take up roles in attending to solving the social conflicts hampering them both in the house and the society.

(IV) THE ROLE OF MEITEI-PANGAL WOMEN IN RELIGION:

The Pangals of Manipur are strict followers of Islam. The religious belief of Islam was based on the teachings of the Holy Quran – the word of God revealed to the prophet Muhammad. The Holy Quran makes it clear that both men and women have the same spiritual gifts. Muslim women in Manipur also follow Islamic religions teachings in their daily lives very strictly. Every Meitei Pangal is supposed to follow recitation of Kalimah "La Ilaha Illa Ilahu : Muhammad Rusulu Ilah." (There is no deity but God, Muhammad is the apostle of God).

Secondly, every Muslim must say his prayers five times daily (Namaz). According to A.J. Shah, this practice "is a devotional exercise which every Muslim is required to render to God at least five times a day, namely at the early morning, midday, afternoon, evening and night"[72]

Thirdly, fasting must be observed by every Muslim during the month of Ramzan. It was necessary for the atonement of sin.

Fourthly, Alms are to be given to the poor and a part of one's income is to be reserved for the state as tax.

Fifthly, every Muslim must make a pilgrimage to Mecca, at least once in his life time.

Moreover, every Muslim is bound to take part in Jihad (Holy War) if he is called upon to do so. But in Manipur the tenets of Jihad (Holy War) is not there in the minds of the Meitei Pangals. Perhaps, the Pangals are adjusted to the Meitei ethos since so many centuries.

In Manipur, the Pangals are expected to follow all the doctrines and laws of Islam but they are not orthodox. Only some pray five times daily but the younger generation finds it hard to follow this practice of praying five times daily.

Children from the age of seven to eight are taught Arabic in the local makhabs (Primary schools) by a Maulvi. Girls are taught hymns for prayer by their mother or female relatives. Sometimes in rural areas a local Maulvi is arranged to teach young girls the proper knowledge of prayers. Religious lessons had to be at home and not outside and the Tutor had to be a woman else the lessons took place with the young girl sitting behind a screen. Sometimes blind tutors were employed to impart religions education to girls so that strict norms of seclusion were not transcended.[37] The conditions under which some girls were sent to school were rather strict. They were transported in strict supervision from the four walls of their homes to the four walls of the school. The concern of the families was that if the girls were seen or exposed to the gaze of the outsiders particularly men it would spell disaster in the sense that it would make their marriage prospect more difficult.[38] But in Manipur, girls enjoyed more freedom and were allowed to come out more freely.

Among the poorer classes, girls were not sent to school as the meager resources at their disposal were allocated to boys' education. Religious education was encouraged because of the teachings of ulema (learned Islamic scholar and teacher). Their teachings were meant to secure a better normal and material life for women and their families. Those women should be able to write and read so that they would know the religious text which was important for both worldly and religious welfare.

According to Daud Sharifa Khanam, the coordinator of the Tamil Nadu Muslim Women's Jamaat Committee, "a mosque for women is my dream. Our women do not have the space to laugh, cry or share thoughts like the men do in mosques. This is not religious struggle. This is a power struggle."[39]

In Manipur, Meitei Pangal women perform prayers in the morning, evening and night whenever they hear the voice of prayer made by the men-folk at nearby mosque.

Muslim women who have visited Mecca are known as 'Hajibi' in Manipur. For the pilgrimage to Mecca, the woman is to be accompanied either by her husband, father, son or brother.

The dead bodies of the Pangals are buried in "Kabarstan" (Grave yard) with Islamic rites. The Pangal woman's nearest relative, be it her mother, sister, mother-in-law, sister-in-law plays a great role in the burial of the dead woman, as they have to do the washing or bathing with water before it is buried. A prayer known as 'Janajah' is performed by the males only. After the burial of the dead body people recite some verses from the Quran for the peace of the soul of the dead person.

Muslim women play their roles well in all aspects of life. But they are not allowed to go to the mosque to pray or enter the mosque. Recently in Lucknow, "it was the Jamiat-ul-Moninath, that first begun training of Muftias, but few of its graduates are practicing clarics. The Hyderabad Jamiat too came out with its batch in the year 2003. The real change came when many of the 100 odd women's mosques in Hyderabad opened their doors to Muftias. Amina Batool, a 17 year old is one of the several young women practicing as Muftias. Women Muftias started delivering Friday sermons in all women mosques, resolving family and marital disperses, confirming divorces and issuing fatwa on current issues such as terrorism."[40] These Muftias do not revolt against established religious practices and beliefs, but they cannot practice at male congregations.

Not a single verse in the Quran, nor a single Hadith forbids a woman from becoming Muftias. Aisha, the Prophet's favourite became a religious authority after his death and served the community. Woman like Amina Batool represent the rise of women power in India's Muslim society. The general lower status of women makes their education the last priority in the family. Any expenditure on them is avoided. Muslim women mostly have more children at an early age. They are tied down by them. The position of Pangal women in Manipur is very low. Purdah or Burkha is used by women of higher class. But purdah system in Manipur depended on the nature of the family and locality. Perhaps the use of purdah name into existence in Manipur after the coming of the maulvis and Maulanas and also after the revival of Islamic religion in Manipur. "Purdah system is a weapon for the physical protection of the women community. A Muslim woman can be a chief of a state, a warrior, an educationist or can be participated in all state affairs."[41]

Islam believes in universal brotherhood of mankind. The prophet laid great emphasis on equality and essential unity of all believers in Islam before the law. Muhammad taught that all Muslims are brothers within the framework of Islam.[42]

In Manipur, the Pangals of Manipur as a whole are Sunnis and they follow Hanafi law, a school of Islamic jurisprudence. All laws are uniform and there is no difference from place to place in the Pangal society. With the forming modernity in Pangal society changes can be seen.

Pangal society is undergoing gradual changes and Muslim women of the state are now aware of their rights and liberty. The Pangal society in Manipur has started establishing religions schools or Madrasa for women. Such schools are at Kairang Heikru Makhong (Ipum Khongban) and also in Irong Mayai Leikai, etc. These programmes are launched under central government schemes. This will certainly help in improving the status of Pangal women in Manipur.

Therefore, it is time that the Pangal women learn the importance of education, higher education and women's empowerment. Women in Pangal society need to mobilize themselves; religious obscurantism and patriarchal controls are some of the burning issues that need to be redressed.

Provision of equality education should be a priority for the government. Vocational training courses and training cum-production centres should be established and encouraged to make girls active in the field of learning and earning. With the help of Rashtriya Mahila Kosh special loans should be provided to the girls of backward communities for completing higher education and vocational training courses. Universalization of education with Mahila Samakhya and Sarva Shiksha Abhiyan is very significant. It should be made compulsory for parents to send their children to school.

Lastly, religious leaders of the Pangal society should take interest and involve in the innovative educational projects because their statements and fatwa carry great significance and the masses are easily convinced be it education or status of women in the society.

The position on reform in personal laws is thus geared towards safeguarding gender interest not as a priority but merely as consideration in the process of safeguarding community interest. Reforms can be brought only by the subjective understanding of Muslim women of their status in the existing laws, recognizing the need for change. Muslim women must be aware of their subordinate legal status within existing personal laws and must engage themselves in the process of change. Due to lack of awareness among Muslim women the process of change is slow due to the poor overall socio economic status of the Muslim community in general and their cultural and religious practices in particular. Therefore, awareness is a necessary condition to enable one to be involved in any process of change.

References

1. Maj. McCulloch; Valley of Manipur (New Delhi, 1950; Reprint.)
2. T.C. Hudson: The Meitheis, 1904; p. 70.
3. Ibungohal and Khelchandra (ed) Cheitharol Kumbaba, Imphal, 1967; p. 21.
4. M.F. Quadir; Muslims of North East India; Souvenir, North East India – 15th Century Hijri Era celebration (Guwahati, 7th & 8th 1981); p. 40.
5. Sayed Ahmed –Muslims in Manipur, Quest for An Identity – July, 2005.
6. Manipuri Muslim Women (Research Study), Salam Irene.
7. O. Tomba : The Need To Rewrite Manipuri History, Imphal 1993; p. 5.
8. Oinam Bhogeshwor, M.A. Janab Khan : Nongmei Puya, Imphal, 1973.
9. *A. Rahman in Manipur Past and Present, Vol.IV of R.K. Sanajaoba;* p. 460.
10. Ipham, M.A. Janab Khan; Manipuri Muslim, Imphal, 1972.
11. R. Brown; Statistical Account of Manipur (Reprint, Delhi-9, 1975); p. 15.
12. Constantine R., Manipur, Maid of the Mountains; Lancer Publishers, 1981; New Delhi; p. 46.
13. *Tokarev, History of Religion, Progress Publishers, Moscow, 1989;*
14. *Interview : Mrs. Laljan Begum, Retired Principal, G.P. Women's College, now member of Manipur State Commission for women on 11 July, 2007.*
15. "Status of Muslim women in Manipur" – Paper presented by Md. Riyas Ahmed Shah.
16. T.P. Hughes : Dictionary of Islam (Rupa, Calcutta, 1988); p.313.
17. S.Q.R. Ilyas (ed), Sim News Bulletin; Vol. V, No. 5 & 6; Aligarh, 1982; p. 21.

18. Quoted by Imtiaz Ahmad in "Jaunty, Kinship and marriage Among Muslims" appeared in Khonthang, 1st issue, August, 1978; pp. 4, 5.
19. S.Q.R. (Op. Cit.) p. 21.
20. Md. Ahmad Ali Shah "A brief historical study of religion and society of the Pangals of Manipur. Dissertation submitted to M.U. for the Award of the Degree of Master of Philosophy.
21. Interview: Mrs. Aman of Keibung Thawan on 10th June, 2007.
22. Dr. K. Kunjani Devi, "Muslim Women's Status in the Family and Society inManipur"; p. 12.
23. Mrs. Laljan Begum, "Muslim Women's Educational Status in Manipur" A seminar paper presented in State Level Seminar on "Status of Muslim Women in Manipur State".
24. The Commentary of father Moserrate Translated and edited by Hoyand & S.N. Bannerjee, London, 1922; p. 209.
25. Islam in India : Impact of Civilizations, Edited by Asghar Ali Engineer, Shipra Publication; pp. 134-135.
26. Ahmad N. Women in Islam, New Delhi, ADH Publishing Corporation, 2003; p. 101.
27. Dr. Md. Kheiruddin Shah, Seminar Paper presented on "The Status of Muslim Women in Manipur State".
28. E.W. Dun, Gazettes of Manipur, Delhi, 1975 (Reprint); p. 16.
29. Socio Economic Survey of MeiteiPangal, 2004; p. 30.
30. Sayed Ahmad: Op.Cit; p. 51.
31. Personal interview : Mrs. Laljan Begum, Member of Manipur State Commissioner for Women on September 3, 2007.
32. Salam Irene: Op. Cit; p. 38.
33. Socio Economic Survey: Op.Cit; pp. 36-40.
34. Wahida Nainar; "Muslim Women's views on personal Laws", (The influence of Socio-Economic Factors), December, 2000.
35. Sayed Ahmed: Op. Cit; p. 54.
36. A.J. Shah, Glimpses of World Religions, Jaico, Bombay, 1990; p. 191.

37. Roy. S., Status of Muslim Women in North India, B.R. Publishing Corporation, Delhi, 1979; p. 50.
38. Ibid, pp. 50-55.
39. The Times of India on 3.5.2005; p. 13.
40. The Telegraph, Guwahati, Thursday 13th August, 2006.
41. Azad Athonba, Muslim Women, The Naharolgi Thoudang, Local News, 3-12-1998.
42. D.R. Dutt: An Outline of World Civilization, New Delhi, 1968; p. 186.

4

Kuki Women's Role

(I) THE ROLE OF KUKI WOMEN IN SOCIETY:

The Kukis are an off-shoot of the Tibeto-Burman race, their original home which many believe to be across the Chin hills. "'Kuki' is the term applied in India and 'chin' is applied in Burma for the same nationality".[1] At first the name sounded incongruous or absurd but when they were continually called by this name they began to accept it. The names which have only 'Denotation' in the beginning later on acquire 'Connotation'.[2] They are also classified as either 'Old Kuki' or 'New Kuki' according to the date when they migrated into Manipur. The term 'Kuki' is a generic word which covers a number of tribes, sub-tribes, clan and sub-clans.

All the tribes have close affinity with each other in terms of language, culture, dress, mode of living, food habits, etc. but they prefer to be identified separately by the names of their respective tribes. Despite their divisions into many tribes, sub-tribes, clans and so on, they have no language barriers. They are able to communicate in their respective dialects.

According to G.A. Grierson, the Kuki Chin is a linguistic sub-family of the Tibeto Burman group comprising Kuki-Chin Mizo (Zo) and the Meitei (Manipuri speakers).[3]

In view of the ethnic conflicts and identity crisis among the different tribes who belong especially to the Non-Naga tribes this research is based on the assumption that there are three major tribes or ethnic communities in Manipur. They are the Meiteis, the Nagas and the Kukis. The term 'Kuki Women' is used in this research work as the term 'Kuki' is used in official records of British, German, Japan and India and all over the world. Unfortunately, there were no monumental inscriptions to trace their past history. Folk tales, oral genealogy, songs, legends and poems etc are the only source materials for the Kukis. The role and action of men has been recorded, but there is no record of Kuki women's role in history writing even when the Kukis fought the British for three years from 1917-1919. Regarding their origin Colonel McCulloch, Political Agent in Manipur for many years in his book "An Account of the valley of Manipur and the Hill tribes reproduced in Carey's "The Chin Hills" in 1859 said "the Khongjais or the Kukis until lately (1859) occupied the hills to the South Koupoous (Khopumphal valley). Not much is known about the Kukis of this period, but their numbers and occasional bloody attacks caused their neighbours to fear them. By these they were driven from their native hills: the task being rendered easier by the internal animosities of the Khongjais themselves. They are now scattered around the valley of Manipur and through the Hills to the north and south of Cachar."[4]

Kuki women are usually short, flat nosed with very rare well cut features. They are strong and lusty and represent unique mongoloid characteristic. "The women have dark yellow brown, dark olive copper and yellow olive skin" Says Tualchin Neihsiel.[5]

Traditionally Kuki women wore nih-san (red-slip) underneath a ponve (wrap-around) which was worn from above the chest. The ornaments included earrings (bilba), necklace (khi) of red and blue colours of cornelian beads. Bracelets and bangles (hahle-chao) are also used by the women. Some girls put a type of ring-shaped earring about one and a half inches in diameter in the ear by stretching the earlobes. It is called 'bilkam'. Of course, some tribes do not use this kind of ornaments. Kuki women traditionally wore their hair in two plaits braided around the head. This hair style is similar to the hair styles of Tibetan women. Once married the girl has to remove the bracelets reluctantly. It is because the older women believe that the use of bracelets by the married women brings bad luck to the family. Rings are now used by the modern Kuki women.

Women in every society play certain roles and enjoy statuses which are different from that of men. The position of women in a society can be identified by examining the roles and activities performed by them in different fields. In the Kuki society there are some activities which are performed exclusively by the women and some that may be performed by both the sexes.

In the traditional society according to K. Kipgen "the duties of a Thadou housewife is much less in comparison with those of her husband. The wife is responsible for the household chores."[6]

Generally, women take the role of nurturing while the men take the role of bread earning. But in the Kuki society women take both the roles. Yet, they have no power and position in the society. From childhood she performs errands for her family. It is the duty of the women to get up early, start the fire, cook food, fetch water, husk the rice and go to the fields for Jhum work. On their return and after doing the same sort of works over and again as in the morning she starts hand spinning work roll cotton threads and weave using traditional tools. For some women who do not have a large family or someone to look after her child (Naodon) she has to carry her baby at the back and do all the works. In body and mind she belonged from her birth till her death to her father, brother, and her husband.

Khamkam studied the position of Paite women as "the mother was loved by all but was not given even position in the home. She occupied the third place in the home. The lot of the mother in the past was deplorable. They work day and night like a servant, yet they were rebuked and insulted rather than praised and honored for the services."[7]

There is a saying, traditionally in Thadou society, that "Numei leh chapang simlou" meaning exclude women and children. The burden of looking after the interests of the family in the home fronts lies on her shoulders. She has every right without consulting anybody of the family to sell animals like pigs, hens and ducks reared by her. Therefore, a close study shows that Kuki women participated in decision making in the privacy of the home and also in the society level, inspite of the fact that her position becomes stable only when she becomes a proud mother of the male inheritors of the lineage and the family properties.

The Kuki society was closely knit and an institution of family was very important. It was casteless society. According to T.S. Gangte, "The class composition of the Kukis and their political organizations were so independent of each other that the Kukis were obsessed with the idea of inter-clan rivalries being helped and fomented by the designing political organization."

Gangte further mentioned that "According to their culture and tradition the social system of the Kukis was so segmented that every individual was made consciously aware that he or she belonged to a particular clan or sub-clan."[8]

The Kukis follow the patriarchal system of family structure. Customary laws and obligation with regard to birth of a child and marriage in the society is extensive. The Kuki society was closely knit and very well organized is made possible by the very important institution of Becha and Tucha. Becha is a person who belongs to a different clan but in the event of any social functions like birth, death, marriage, etc. the Becha assumes the "responsibilities of managerial work" and implements the decision of the head of the family on his behalf. However, some old Kuki groups like the Chiru, Kom, Chothe etc. the 'Becha' system is not practiced but in its place the maternal uncle is given due importance in all similar matters.[9]

In the traditional Kuki society the maternal bond is not broken as there are many cultural rites and ceremonies which are observed even after a woman got married and left her maternal home.

It is the Tucha Sungao relation which have become an indispensable part of the social life of the Kukis 'Nephew' in Kuki language is 'Tu' and a 'child' of one's sister is 'cha'. Therefore, Tucha means a child born of a sister and in turn the mother's brother's children are called Sung-gao. The Tucha Sung-gao relationship is purely based on blood connections which expresses loyalty and solidarity of the blood relationship and mutual voluntary obligation. It is a by-product of matrimonial alliance and can have no other consideration whatsoever. The position of a Sung-gao in relation to his tucha is nothing but to give. In a society where mother's brother's daughter's marriage is preferred, the Sung-gao relative of an ego occupies a high position. Also, the Sung-gao relative (the eldest son) has the right to claim the 'Long-man' (death price or corpse price) of his 'Tute' who were born of his sister. This death price is taken not as a punishment, but as proof of the love bond relationship between the brother's and sister's children. This signifies the good will of the Tute and opens the door for cross-cousin marriage called "Neite-Kilah" (maternal uncle's daughter). The Kukis believed that this form of marriage ensures good health for the married couple and their children and it also establishes a continuous and permanent link between two groups of families. Inspite of traditional prescription for this type of Neinu-Neipa marriage, its popularity among the younger generation is on the wane. The new generations of youths marry outside the clan group.

In the marriage system of the Kukis whatever the type of marriage, a bride price has to be paid by the boy's side to the girl's family. It varies from clan to clan. This bride price is said to have a social value as it is not to be paid in full even if one is able to do so. Bride-price, however, does not lower down the status of women in Kuki society. It rather enhances her status in as much as an accomplished bride fetches higher bride-price. The bride price received is matched by the dowry given by the parents. The standard of the dowry and the bridal feast given by the bride's parents enhances her prestige among her friends and among women in general. It appears to be a safety value for good economic relations between the wife given and wife-taker family, besides guarantying good conduct of the bride whose failure to satisfy the groom may lead to the forfeiture of the bride price to be received by the wife giving family. It also implies that the man should have obligation, love, respect, etc for his wife and her relatives. It is to build a good relation with his wife's side.

"The unpaid portion" of the bride-price "implies that his wife and relatives are precious as the precious stones and assets yet to be paid".[10]

Gangte further suggested two reasons for paying the bride-price. One is for compensation to the economic loss of the girl's family as she is the main pillar of the family's economy. The other reason is that she is the bearer of children for the expansion of family line of generation. Here one can understand one of the important roles played by Kuki Women. Traditionally, divorce was allowed. If a man divorces his wife without any cause, he does not get back the bride price he had paid and he is also fined one Mithun as Daman (Divorce). If it is the woman who divorce her husband, the husband can take back the bride price he had paid to her. There is a saying in Kuki which shows that a husband could divorce his wife at any time. It says "Numei Phalou le honpal phalou chu khel ding mong ahi" which means a bad wife and a bad fence can always be replaced.

There is another unique custom at the death time of the Kukis where women are given prominent place. If a man has paid the full price for his wife during marriage he has on her death and the death of her sons to pay a further sum called Long-man[11] (corpse price) to the nearest male relative. This shows an important position held by Kuki women in the family. Therefore, in the Tucha – Sung-gao relation the bride price and Longman have social values in relation to women.

Traditionally, Kuki women were not socially aware. By observing the ethnological ways of the Kuki tribe one can safely assume that a Kuki woman within her family configuration and social setting remains a "patriarchal woman". A patriarchal woman, in the words of Lois Tyson,[12] can be defined as "a woman that has internalized the norms and values of patriarchy".

Patriarchy can be defined in short, as any culture that privileges men by promoting traditional gender roles. Traditional gender roles cast men as rational, strong, protective and decisive and on the other hand they cast women as emotionally (irrational) weak, nurturing and submissive. The cultural habit of patriarchal dominance as universal still play an important role in successfully excluding women from equal access to leadership and decision making positions both in the family and beyond the household. However, in contemporary times considerable transformation have begun to surface both within the four walls of the home and in the society.

By observing the nuances of fluctuating family values, fluid inter-personal relationships and the influence as well as the inevitable affects of western science and capitalism, in other words industrialization, Kuki women no longer hesitate to in attempting to negotiate their traditional feminity with the needs of modern times which is an ever-pressing reality.

Kuki women started to take part in movements which are burning topics of the present society, be it political, social and economic issues of the society from time to time. They no longer remained silent spectators when anti state violence against women and anti Manipuri activities threatened their state Manipur. In August 4, 1997 when OCTIM (Organising Committee of Territorial Integrity of Manipur) organized a mass rally Kuki women also joined the mass rally. Again they, in their traditional dresses, also participated in the rally organized both by the AMKIL (Apunba Manipur Kanba Ima Lup) and NIPCO (National Identity Protection Committee) on 28th September, 2000. Kuki women for Human Rights Network Manipur and Kuki Mothers Association condemned the uncivilized act of the security forces for firing upon anti cease fire protestors on (June 18th) 2001. Even the Human Rights Network also expressed their strong opinion for basic rights of the people.

Today, Kuki society will no longer castigate her like it would have years ago if she wished to pursue "unwomanly" vocation in present times. The future looks bright for young, budding Kuki women who are ready to step out of their societal 'cocooning'.

(II) KUKI WOMEN'S ROLE IN POLITICS:

The traditional political system of the Kukis centres on chiefship. The chief is the central figure in the political administration of the Kukis. The village chief called 'Hao-sa' is the administrative head of the village and governs in accordance with customary law. "Chieftainship" is a very powerful secular institution based on Kinship structure for the purpose of village administration which is the highest and independent political unit.[13]

A Kuki chief is so powerful within his village jurisdiction that according to Kuki custom everything in a village belongs to the chief, who can demand anything he requires. The Kukis are patrilineal, and descent is based on the uni-lineal principle and authority is determined from father to son. As such the eldest or the youngest son is the heir apparent. A chief remains a chief throughout his life. Goswami wrote that "Chief among the Kukis should be the one who is the strongest, the wealthiest and the eldest man in the family".[14] In case of the Lushais, however, it has been changed from youngest to eldest in recent times.[15]

John Macrae has also written that "each tribe is under the immediate command of its own particular chief, whose word is law, in peace and war and who has the power of life and death".[16]

The chief performed judiciary, executive and legislative functions in the day to day administration of the village in consultation with his council of ministers called Semang Pachong (Councillors). The number of Semang Pachong varies from village to village. The villagers have to pay a tribute called Changseo (basket of paddy) annually to the chief after the harvest, and Samaal (right hind leg of animal) killed in any hunting expedition.

The chief also nominates from the poor minority clan members to hold minor offices such as Lhangsam in the Council so that there is no discrimination among the villagers. His council of ministers remain in office as long as they enjoy the pleasure of the Haosa (chief).

N. Chatterjee describes the Kuki chief's power as one "who lived in the village were looked upon as his own children. He was bound to help them in their adversaries /Counsel them in their difficulties, reward them in their achievement and punished them when they were found guilty of misdeeds and infring."[17]

The Chief's house generally served as the court of the village. All cases were decided with the help of the village elders and the Councillors, according to the customary laws and practices. Since monetary system was not known in the traditional society fines were exacted in kind such as a jar of Ju (rice beer) fowls, pigs, Mithun, etc. Trials of dispute like theft, land dispute, assault and seducement were considered as small crimes, while incest, sexual relationship with another's wife, one's own brothers, sisters, father, daughter, sons or mother were considered as biggest crimes in the Kuki society. However, killing of an enemy or destruction of enemy's property is not considered criminal acts according to the Kuki customary laws. All disputes are settled in the house of the village chief.

Thus, the chief's house is constructed as largely as possible. The chief, apart from appointing the Semang Pachong (Council of Ministers) appointed Lhangsampa (Convenor of the Council), Kho Thempu (village priest) now-a-days replaced by the Church Pastor, Thih Khengpa (Blacksmith) Lom Haosa (Chief of the village Corps) and Becha and Tucha of the Haosa (village chief). The 'Haosa' howsoever, absolute his right over the land might be normally allows in consultation with his Council of Ministers.[18]

Regarding the members of the Council, the Chief has a group of elders nominated and retained by him at his pleasure though in this selection he gives a fair representation to the various clans in this village.[19]

Today, with the introduction of the Village Authority Act, 1956 in Manipur the village organisation under the leadership of the Haosa (Village Chief) has changed in its structure and function. According to this Act the Haosa is the Chief Ex-Officio Chairman of the village authorities. The members are no longer nominated by the Chief but are elected by the villagers themselves.

The new Act brought in elements of democratic principles in the constitution of the village authorities where members were earlier nominated they are now to be elected. A drastic change had taken place in the role of customary laws applicable in the society.[20]

Traditionally, Kuki women had no role to play in politics especially in the village administration. Women were not allowed to utter even a word in the meetings of Haosa-upa (village elders). Their role was only to distribute red-tea in the meetings. Women's participation in village Councils was very limited. Widows having no son were allowed to attend the annual village meeting but she was not allowed to have an affective say in any important matter.

Women's participation in the traditional political organisation was very little as it was considered to be an exclusive domain for their male counterparts only. Chiefs or Chairman of a village Council are only male.

However, a striking thing we discovered from our empirical research is that there are some women who hold Chieftainship or Chairmanship of the village Council after the death of their husbands. More strikingly, one of them had held chieftainship for about 15 years. She is Mrs. Lamkhoneng Haokip of Vakan Village, Manipur from (1985-2000). Another woman named Vahjaneng Mate of Tengnoupal village of Chandel District also holds chieftainship after her husband's death.[21] Mrs. Lhaikhohoi Haokip of Kotlen Village, New Cachar road (Senapati District) and Mrs. Nemjating Gangte[22] of Santing Village in Churachandpur District hold chieftainship since 1992 till date. In Chandel district itself there are four women chiefs.

Apart from Mrs. Vahjaning Mate, Miss Ating (Christina) Haokip, daughter of L. Jamson Haokip became the chief of Saivom Village. Villages like Bongli and Chahmol of Machi block in Chandel District are all headed by women like Neikhochong Haokip and Vahneng Haokip respectively.[23] In the village Council women were included. For example, in Molnom village, Churachandpur district Mrs. Ngainei, wife of Ngangam Haokip and Mrs. Thenneng, wife of Rev. L.Lhunkholet were elected (in 2007) as Village Local Committee members.

These are some of the exceptional examples of women who take part in the decision making of the village administration.

In modern politics women have started involving themselves in casting votes and also some have stood for political leadership. Kuki women, like their other communities, enjoyed adult franchise for the first time in 1948. They have started participating in the political process of the state both as voters and candidates. And the number of voters always out numbered men voters. Mrs. Lhingjaneng Gangte was nominated as Member of the Territorial Council from 1957 to 1963 and nominated to the territorial Assembly from 1963-1969. There was also another woman who was nominated along with Mrs. Lhingjaneng Gangte. She was Mrs. Akim Angnal. In the mid term Assembly Election in 1974, Mrs. Lhingjaneng Gangte contested from Saikot constituency, but was defeated. Mrs. Lhingjaneng Gangte also received "Padma Shree Award" from the Indian Government (an award given to an outstanding person).[24]

In the Parliamentary election Miss Kim Gangte was elected as Member of Parliament in 1998, as a C.P.I. Candidate. Many Kuki women contested for the assembly seats but could not succeed due to provisional lack of confidence on women's leadership by the people.

For rural women in Manipur political participation is a far distant dream. Because, there is no Panchayati Raj system in all the hill districts and District Autonomous Councils have been defunct.

The general attitude of males towards inclusion of women as authority member is not encouraging. Moreover, women in the hills are generally not concerned with this issue except for a few enlightened women who discuss the matter occasionally in an informal discussion.[25]

Individual women progressing upwards on their own merits, because of personality factors or connections or particular competencies, do not necessarily carry women's concerns, women's issues or interests unless these issues enter the political process. Women, generally, are also ignorant of their rights and also the importance of women's participation in decision making bodies and levels. The important role placed by Kuki women as a decision maker can be seen even during the Anglo Kuki War of Independence of 1917-1919.

It was the Kuki women who guarded the villages, looked after their homes and families. They suffered silently the pangs of separation from their loved ones when their men folk went to war against the British. It is unimaginable the hardship, the emotional trauma they must have faced when the British took their men for labour corps to France. According to T. Lunkim, it was nothing but Chieftainship which fought against the British.[26]

Not only this, the Kuki women suffered untold miseries during and after the war when the Kuki Chiefs and leaders of the war were imprisoned and punished. Villages suspected to have been involved in abetting and sheltering the so called "Rebels" during the war were burnt down. It was the woman and children who suffered most and the loss of life on the part of the Kukis might perhaps be no less than that of the government though the exact figure of the dead and wounded on the side of the Kukis are not available. These brave women who went through untold miseries can be called "forgotten heroines" of the Anglo Kuki war of Independence of 1917 because they are the ones who bravely put on their shoulder the responsibilities of guarding their villages, supplying food to the men, looking after the wounded warriors etc. And also "for the Kuki warriors asking them to go to France simply as labourers in the war front was considered an insult of the highest degree."[127] Their pride must have been hurt when their women took over as a decision making bodies in the village administration and in their homes for the proud Kuki warriors who thought that "menial labour falls within the realms of women's domain".[28]

The struggle of the Kukis for freedom and independence under the British rule in Manipur continued even after their defeat in Anglo Kuki war of 1917-19.

Kuki men and women joined the INA (Indian National Army) forces and served in intelligence as reporters, guides, sepoys and others.

Interestingly the Kukis were not totally dependent upon the British supplies of arms and ammunitions. But the gifted skills of the villagers enabled them to produce simple forms of weaponry tools and implements for both aggressive and defensive purposes. Consequently the chiefs' fighting-men possessed guns (which had flint-locks ......). They manufactured their own gun powder.[29]

In 1916, Rules for administration of the hill areas were modified.[30]

Prof. Laldena has remarked that "regarding the administration of the hill people, the British assumed the role of a 'Saviour' minus a redeeming power."[31]

Undue collection of money from the hill village and the Lambus were also responsible in no small measure for out break of the Kuki Rebellion".[32]

The British authorities assumed the administration of the hill tribes after the Anglo Kuki war and established their direct control over the latter.[33] They justified their action on the ground that only by maintaining a decent standard of administration can peace be preserved.[34] History shows that Manipuris can not and will not give the hills an administration of the standard to which they are both entitled and now accustomed".[35] The Kuki Inn which stands in the heart of Imphal city is a living testimony of brave Kuki warriors.

In 1944, a Kuki woman named Hoijakim and her husband Longjangam Kuki carried the letter of Netaji Subhas Chandra Bose to Imphal and delivered to Thokchom Angou Singh. It was suggested by Dr. Gulabjao who was posted at Sugnu during that time. They also met Potsangbam Tomal Singh and Laishram Kanhai before they return back."[36] Mrs. Hoijakim and her husband acted as a spy for the Indian National Army forces in Manipur, thereby extending her assistance in the freedom movement against the British rule.

Netaji and his INA with the slogan "Chalo Delhi" marched towards Delhi from Singapore by crossing Burma border on the 14th April, 1944. The INA under the leadership of Col. S.A. Malik hoisted the Tri-colour flag for the first time on the sacred soil of liberated area at Moirang.

In fact, the soil of 'Moirang' was sanctified by the blood and tears of the Indo-Japanese forces.[37]

Onkholet Haokip also known as Japan Pakang followed the Japanese upto Japan as he could not stay in his own land in the face of enemy's domination.

The British also constructed roads in the hills connecting the administrative headquarters, which was established after the Anglo-Kuki War of 1917-1919. Even before the Anglo Kuki War, the road from Imphal to Moreh was constructed under the supervision of Lt. Raban and it was completed in 1881.[38]

Kuki customs, culture and traditions establish the superiority of men over women. But the improvement through education has changed the relationship of Kuki man and woman and brought about the emancipation of women in Kuki society. Now-a-days, Kuki women are faring as well as their male counterparts in their academic and professional pursuits. Kuki society has become more liberal and tolerant than it was before.

(III) KUKI WOMEN'S ROLE IN ECONOMY

The main occupation of the Kukis is agriculture, practised in its traditional form, terrace and jhum cultivation. They settled in almost all the entire hill areas of Manipur and the adjoining regions of the North-eastern India, Myanmar and Bangladesh. "The Kukis like Kom, Anal, Hmar, Vaiphei, Gangte, Koireng, Chothe, Chiru, Purum, Hiroi Lamgang, Mayon, Monshang, etc. are surmised to have arrived in Manipur during 14th century to 15th century A.D.[39] They were followed by Thadou, Khongsais and his cognate groups into the region at the end of 16th century and beginning of 17th century. The Kukis shifted from one place to another in search of suitable terrain for settlement. The Kukis, like other tribes solely depended on mode of Agricultural economy. In as far as Jhuming cultivation is concerned majority of the Kuki tribes sow their seeds without upturning the soil.[40]

The Kuki women work side by side their husbands in the fields. Their source of livelihood is provided by the land they inhabit and the forest around them. With the primitive technology at their command they feel at home in the midst of forest life which is inseparable from high landish society. They form groups called 'Lom' where they work together taking turns to work in their fields. 'Lom' is said to be one of the most important organisation concerned with the economic relations among the Kukis. The literal meaning of lom is understood as collective labour force. This collective service gives the Kuki women a sense of responsibility, fraternity and peaceful co-existence among them. This contribute greatly to the socio-economic development of the village in particular and the society in general. This Lom system also helps the poor and needy people like the widows. Thus Lom was practised by the Kukis and continued to be practiced even upto the present day.

Kuki women cultivated various types of crops by using an implement of dibbling stick made of bamboo or wood and a small hoe called 'Tucha' by digging the soil and inserting the seed therein covered with the soil. Weeding is done on the basis of the growth of the weeds. Other than rice, Kuki women cultivated varieties of cash crops like cucumber, maize, beans, gourds, ginger, turmeric, taro or yam locally known as (Paan or Baal) etc. In Manipur Jhum is heavily practised in the areas where the Kukis inhabited predominantly than the areas inhabited by their Naga or Meitei counterparts.[41]

According to Sanajaoba "The Naga and Kuki tribals also cultivate cotton in large quantities in various parts of hill areas which were sold in several urban centres including Imphal."[42] He further mentioned that cotton became the main source of income for many Kuki household as a cash crop, But "in the interior highlands except for self consumption, the Kuki jhumists neglected cash crops due to lack of transport and marketing facilities. The Kuki women are accustomed to collecting wild fruits, bamboo shoot, vegetables and it is their duty to sell them in the market with that small amount of money they get they buy food required for their families.

Kuki women also started coming to the market in Imphal to sell their vegetables grown in their own fields. There are women who open small shops by selling meat, tea or second hand clothes in Imphal areas and also in the hill areas. They also formed themselves into societies or self-help groups. These societies have at least 20 women in each group. They focus on making the best use of the local resources and making the maximum possible uses. Since, there is a great availability of fruits like oranges, pineapples, lemon, passion fruits, etc. they make squashes, jams, achar, etc and sell them in the market. The profit they distributed among themselves, thereby contributing her share in the economy of the family. The traditional economy of the Kukis is subsistence economy. They manufactured almost anything from bamboo baskets to gunpowder for their socio economic requirements.

Kuki women are expected to learn the art of weaving from childhood. In the past women who are expert in the art of weaving were considered to be better brides as her services strengthened the domestic economic condition. Kuki "Dresses in general are the identity of a nation or a tribe. Dresses are like the unwritten code where by a man's social status and culture can be determined. The Kuki ways of dressing are often artistic, well adapted to the working condition of the hills. Not only the Kukis but the different tribes of the Nagas also have special shawls with symbols of animals, objects etc. for their festive occasion."[43]

To exploit their talents, the Kukis did careful handicraft work and artistic designs. This reflected their love, affection and recognition of their belief and culture. These beautiful shawls and wrap around are much in demands among the elite class of the Kuki women. Patterns and designs of some of the Kukis like the Thadous are taken from the colours of animals like Python, fish bone, elephant knee, jungle bamboo tube, mortar etc. It is believed that a lady who operates the work of weaving without performing any ritual or offering will not last long. Since there was no major industries among the hill tribes most of their day to day domestic needs were met by themselves. Pottery making was considered the work of women folk among the Kukis.

Rochunga Pudaite writes that "When the village site was selected, great importance was attached to the availability is the Bubel Khur's pit. A limited variety like Bubel (rice-cooking pot) Meh-bel (curry-cooking pot) An Kuang (covering and eating plates) Ngaubel (distillation for fermenting rice beer) and Zubel (rice-beer pot) were made. The largest varieties were the Zubel and Ngaubel which contained between two to five gallons. A smaller variety called Tuk-bel (smoking pipe) of different shapes and sizes were also made and these were mainly for women young girls before marriageable age learnt to do it".[44]

The Kuki women used to sell rice-beer which was liked by all. But this custom is not in practice now as most of the Kukis have converted to Christianity. It is used at times of religious ceremonies and social functions. Tobacco smoking is common both among men and women in the Kuki society.

The most popular smoke used in the traditional days was Tuibuh (Tobacco juice) and Dumphol and Dum-mom are

Tobacco leaves. The Kukis are rarely seen without a pipe in their mouth. In Churachandpur district mostly women comes to the market and sells tuibuh. With such a small amount of money she gets from selling this tobacco juice she makes her contribution in the maintenance of her family. Hudson described in his own words the habits of smoking as inducing strength while walking with one of his Kuki counterpart

"I have traveled with Kukis who ate nothing all day but kept up their strength by constant sips of this juice, which they retained in the mouth not more than three minutes at a time."[45]

Like any other tribal societies belonging to different clans the Kuki women are expected to engage themselves in lighter part of the domestic works whereas the more difficult jobs are done by their male counterparts. Felling down trees, clearing the thick jungles, house construction, hunting, fishing in deep water, etc are left for the men.

Spinning, weaving, cooking etc. are exclusively women's domain. Rearing of poultry and pigs is equally a feminine activity and she also has every right without consulting anyone to sell animals reared by her. In exceptional cases, widows without adult sons may engage in activities which are normally preserved as male activity. Like the Meiteis there are also some women who spend their days toiling hard in the river banks to gather sand and shingles working for long hours with lots of physical exertion; they are given a meager sum for the day just to sustain their daily requirement.

In the first half of 20th Century under colonial economy rice became a prospective commercial crop in Manipur. Consequently, the British authorities began to take interest in expanding terrace cultivation.[46]

Besides, Potato cultivation by Kukis and Nagas in the hills being successful was encouraged by the British.[47]

Traditionally, the only trade known among the Kukis was barter which was carried out within the village circle. The only assignment in which they were engaged in their day to day life was Vaikon/Loukon (field appointment). Money system of trade and commerce was not known until they came in contact with other neighbouring tribes. The advent of British gave the Kukis the knowledge of currency system. The Kukis in particular were self-sufficient in their day to day life. They had no other concerns other than agricultural activities in connection with their economy. But things have changed with the coming of the British. Western education opened the eyes of the Kukis and they realized the importance of having material possessions and the importance of education. In a Kuki family the presence of one talented and skillful woman could extend her support economically, to the whole family. The labour inputs and time spent by both male and female is comparatively the same with that of agricultural activities. Even though the Kukis in the past had limited needs and wants they had trade relationship with the Meiteis and 'hill traders were well developed who traded in plantain leaves, cotton cane, bamboo goods, beads, charcoal products, etc."[48]

The Kukis led a measurable socio-economic life more so during and after the Anglo Kuki War, 1917-1919. The British had exploited their man power and resources for shipment during the First World War 1914-1917. The continuance of the war for more than two years meant complete draining away of their economic resources. Since the Kukis could not go to the fields, there was a total breakdown of economy. As a result the starving Kuki warriors surrendered to the British. The introduction of money economy and the expansion of markets had a far reaching impact on the socio-economic life of the Kukis. People began to think of producing goods to sell in the markets and earn money. In this also it is the women folk who took larger share of the responsibility in earning money and profit.

Now-a-days, Kuki women in many cases are also the bread earner of the family. There are many educated Kuki women working as Government employees in different departments of the Manipur Government. Educated women working in different fields contribute much to the family's income thereby raising the status of the family.

Unfortunately, during the early 1990's on account of the so-called ethnic cleansing of the NSCN-IM the economic condition of the Kukis worsened. Many Kuki women became widowed and large number of children wereorphaned and rendered homeless. The Kukis became landless and were reduced to a mere wage earner or hire labourers, which was unknown in the past. To sustain their daily needs they took up different occupations not by choice but out of necessity. Many young girls became prostitutes and many youth became drug addicts because the kind of ethnic tension led to local migration which resulted in economic instability. It is true that in the Kuki society there are some who belongs to the creamy layer of the society but in general for the majority of the Kukis to reach the standard of living as enjoyed by the advanced communities may take several decades.

Like any tribal society Kuki society is also patriarchal in which women have no say over inheritance of property. It is unfortunate to note that in spite of their tremendous contribution to the family income they have no right of inheritance. Our research has shown that a few thoughtful parents do share their property among daughters and sons. With the introduction of Self-Help Groups by N.G.Os Kuki women are now introduced to awareness programmes ranging from conflict resolution to prevention of HIV/AIDS, how to stand on their own feet, how to become economically independent, and Kuki women are on their way to viewing the world with new eyes.

(IV) ROLE OF KUKI WOMEN IN SPORTS

In the Kuki society men are more advanced than women in the field of sports. In the 1950s and 1960s many Kuki women started playing Hockey under the Kuki sporting Club. These women who played Hockey were :

1. Mrs. Lamkhonei Sitlhou. (She was the Captain).
2. Mrs. Mami Kipgen.
3. Mrs. Tingkholam Gangte.
4. Mrs. Phalkhoneng Haokip.
5. Mrs. Chinnu Kipgen.
6. Mrs. Nengkhochong Sitlhou.
7. Mrs. Lhingneikim Kipgen.
8. Mrs. Nempi Tungnung.
9. Mrs. Lhingboi Gangte.

Unfortunately, after them no Kuki women played Hockey again.

Again, in 1970s and 1980s many young Kuki girls took interest in sports again and they also played Basket ball for the Kuki sporting Club as well as for the State of Manipur. They were :

1. Miss Ngaineikim Kipgen,
2. Miss Achong Haokip,
3. Miss Akim Haokip,
4. Miss Achin Haokip.
5. Miss Alhing Haokip.
6. Miss Zoumoun Thangzom,
7. Miss Nengshi Kipgen.
8. Miss Veikhokim Gangte.

These bright young Kuki girls represented their college, i.e. G.P. Women's College and played Basket ball for the State as well at the National level.

Even in football Kuki women like Miss Tingcha Singsit (1980s to 1990s) and Miss Lhingboi Misao became famous football players among the Kuki women. In the field of Boxing, Mary Kom became a household name in the national level as well as international level.[49]

Therefore, given the chance Kuki women can compete and excel in any field, be it politics, administration, business, education and sports. To conclude, it would not be wrong to state that education is the primary need of the moment. A native woman can radicalize her view points and liberalize her ways of living without even having to compromise her integrity and her dignity. Educated women are more likely to be aware of their personal rights, political rights and professional aspirations, and gain access to knowledge, inventions and transformation. Therefore, encouragement should be given to young girls without any partiality.[50]

(V) KUKI WOMEN'S ROLE IN RELIGION

Religion forms the backbone of the beliefs and practices in the Kuki social structure. These traditional religions of the Kukis is said to be animism in which all objects like animals, plants, mountains, stones, rivers, etc. are believed to have souls. Therefore, the Kukis believed that fertility of the soil, rain or drought, the success and failure of crops depended upon the incantations and rituals of a Thempu (*priest*) more than human effort. His power and functions are very important in the day to day life of the animists Kukis. The Kukis believed in the existence of a super natural God called "Chung Pathen" or "Chung Mangpa" meaning God of heaven who made the universe and who is believed to live in heaven. The belief in the existence of a chief God called 'Pathen' did not prevent them from believing in a number of minor gods and goddesses. But this belief did not interfere in the daily affairs of human beings nor did He demand sacrifices from the people. This perhaps may be the reason why Chung Pathen (*Supreme God*) was ignored and the early Kuki was totally absorbed in the appeasement of the evil spirit (*Noi Mungpa*).

This belief resulted in the performance of elaborate rites and rituals which became their religion and way of life. Traditionally, the Thiempu or Village Priest was considered to be the servant of God, and all sacrifices, and religious matters were performed by him.

In the course of their life journey, the Kukis developed a religion called 'Indoi' – worship (house-deity). If one analyses the components of this indoi, it is nothing but an attempt by men to bring the surrounding nature into harmony with himself and members of his family and thereby ensure abundance, health and prosperity to the family.

According to the Kukis the installation of In-doi brings the surrounding nature into harmonious existence with members of the family having its In-doi installed.[51]

Indoi of the Kukis is a bundle of charms made by the Thempu (witch doctor or priest) who has the requisite knowledge of incantation.

The Indoi consists of seven objects bound with a single cord to a bamboo spike, some of the objects being ornamented with feathers from a white cock. The spike is thrust into the porch of the house. For the purpose of making a new Indoi (*house-deity*) the following are required :-

1. A pig's skull : to confer vigor and fertility, and protection from diseases.
2. A goat's horn : to confer beauty and strength.
3. A small portion of a gourd : to confer plenty of food and drink.
4. A piece of 'Shething' and 'Thinga' (*a kind of special trees for this purpose*).
5. A small bamboo knife 'Chempong' : to ensure safety from all dangers.

6. A miniature gourd containing water and seeds : to ensure safety from evil spirits.
7. A circular jar (*Belval*) : to ensure wealth.

The above articles are bound together by a single cord fibre called Khaopi (*a bark of a special tree that makes an excellent rope*). This rope symbolizes strength for body and good health. A sword and spear and a woman's brass wristlet called 'Chaop' are given to the priest. The priest takes a small bit of each of the above and with the spear, dao and wristlet in his hands makes an incantation. The prayer is mainly for the house owner for whom the house magic or Indoi is made. Actually, the white cock's feathers symbolizes light and life as the Kukis had escaped from darkness that once covered the whole world for seven days when many Kukis perished in the darkness.[52]

The Thempu continues to bless the owner of the house for whom the Indoi is made. He blesses him for wealth, longevity, prosperity and also prays that the householder may be blessed with many sons and daughters. Thus, the Indoi become an indispensable household deity for safeguarding its inmates.

Shaw terms indoi as the house magic, a bundle of charms which is made either by the Thempu (*Priest*) or by another person who has requisite knowledge of what is required.

The Kukis also practiced ancestor worship in pre-Christian times. "The belief that spirits of the ancestors abound within the premises of the house and participates in their midst further adds to their enthusiasm."[53]

The Mizos called this Rao-Chheak. The similarities in the animistic religions, practices among the Kuki-chin group, can also be seen in the case of ancestor worship.[54] This shows that ancestors are not forgotten by the Kukis because they believed that the spirits of ancestors aided mortals in attaining blessings from Pathen, the Supreme God.

Further, the Kukis believed that the Indoi (house deity) was said to be a gift to Mr. and Mrs. Hangsing from spirits who kidnapped their daughter for a wife. Perhaps Mr. Hangsing was the first Kuki to make Indoi which made him rich and powerful.

In due course of time, several distinct festivals were developed in the social life of the Kukis to observe one's achievements such as Sa-ai (ritual performed by great hunters to gain complete dominance over the spirits of the killed animals); Chang Cha Kou (inviting paddy spirit); Chang Nungah (a rare variety of rice plant growing sparsely along with the rice plant). A ritual is performed by slaughtering a cock or hen, because the Kukis believe that this type of plants help increase the fertility of the field and also augments production. When such paddy plants grow in the midst of the actual paddy plants these are very carefully preserved even after the harvest.[55]

Besides Sa-ai, Chaang-ai and Gal-ai are also performed by the Kukis in commemoration of a soul killed at war. It is believed that if no ritual is performed, the slayer is likely to go mad.

Among the religious ceremony Hun (religious ceremony) involved family members and the whole villagers once a year in the months of March or April when new leaves starts coming out from different trees. This ritual is led by the village Thempu (priest). On these days each and every household's indoi/Doibom (household deity) is placed in front of their courtyard and a post called Shi-Khom is erected in front of the house. The post bears two branches of different length, one at the top and the other at the bottom. Two pots of wine, each pot contributed by husband and the wife are hung on the branches. The wine of the husband is taken by the household members only but the wife's wine is served to all visitors. Each household prepare a pot of wine and soft bread made of powdered rice and killed a white cock for the feast which is to be taken by the father, mother, the priest and the village chief. This worshipping of god by killing a white cock is done in order to get prosperity from their God called Chung Pathen / Chung Mangpa.

Chon is also a ritual performed by great hunters and warriors. Only a person who had performed Sa-ai three times can perform the Chon ritual. "The Chon ritual as a household ceremony and not regular offerings like other rituals and that tradition does not fix any particular day or moon for the ceremony. The day is fixed in reference with the solar system. In most cases, it is held during winter, probably to avoid the rain, usually on a full moon day".[56]

Dai-phu (agricultural rites and rituals) is performed to appease the demon and evil spirits which are living in that particular field.

Kho-geh (community preventive ritual) is observed to prevent epidemics like Cholera, diarrhea, etc. This ritual is performed by the Thempu in the presence of the Semang Pachong in the village cemetery called Kho-Moul.

The Kukis also observe one day called Umnit/Sahnit (holiday observe for agricultural activities) when unnatural death (Thi-se) like Thinga-lha (*death by falling from tree*); Tui-a-Thi (*drowned in water*); Thal-a-thi (*death from guns or weapons*); Kikhai lih (*Suicide by hanging self*); Kol-a-Kitang (*falling from cliff*) occurred. It is believed that if such days are not observed the incident is expected to fall on to the person who does not observe the day.

According to the tradition of the Kukis, when a person dies a number of religious and customary formalities are performed as Kitom (*outburst of Anger*) is performed by the Tuhcha of the death family. This is done to challenge the Killer - Death through expression of defiance.[57]

Lang-lap is another ritual performed by the Kukis when important persons like Hao-sa, Semang Pachong and people who performed Sa-ai and Chon rituals die. The dead body is kept for three to seven days on a bamboo platform called Lang. This ritual is called Langa-Lap. It is believed that after this ritual the soul of the dead person ascends directly to the Mithi-Kho (*abode of the death*) without any disturbance. If not the Khul Samnu (*female demon*) would capture the corpse and keep it as her slave. The Kukis believed in the existence of soul after death. The Kuki ancestors believed that the soul of every dead Kuki passed through the mountain which lay between Chin-Hills in Burma and Mizoram in India. When the soul passed through these ranges it would go to the other world called Mithikho (*abode of the death*).

Another feature common among the Kuki Chin groups is the practice of head-hunting because additional head for the Kukis meant an additional slave for the soul at Mithi-Kho. It was simply an eligibility requirement for a smooth passage to God. Animist Kukis found nothing wrong in this practice in pre-Christian times. Reasons for the practice of head hunting varied from tribe to tribe, village to village. Another reason for head hunting is said to have been connected with vengeance. Therefore, the Priest (*Thempu*) performed rituals before the party left for war or raid. In the practice of head hunting according to Thangkim Haolai the highest value was placed on the child's head, male or female, a head hunter must practically enter the enemies' village. Next in value is that of a woman since this would mean going very near to the village. After that comes the head of the known warrior of the enemy. The least value was an ordinary man or youth. This cruel custom before the advent of Christianity created disunity, mistrust and fighting among different tribes and clans.

Traditionally, in every Kuki village administration every village had Kho-Thempu (Village priest). This Kho-Thempu is counted as one of the members of the council of ministers. And as the chief has nothing to do with the rituals in the religious functions, the priests or the Thempu was all in all.[58]

As a custom, the Kuki women do not hold any priestly office but there are instances of un-official priestesses or sorceress, for example, Mrs. Lamkhoneng Changsan was a priestess (Thempi) and functioned like other male priests in Taizawl village, N.C. Hills, Assam.[59]

Others are Mrs. Vahshi, wife of Jampao Sitlhou of Ponlen Village, Sadar Hills and Vahhoi, wife of Khaitong Kholhou of Karakhun village, Sadar Hills, Manipur.[60]

There are also other instances, such as, Thongkholun nu of Joupi village knew 'Themthi' (incantation used by Thempu) while performing sacrifices for the sick and people who were in dire need of her help. Such type of priestess usually performed priestly function when there was no male and when people were in need. Rev. Seikholet Singson, the first ordained Minister among the Kuki Christians says that usually the priest teaches his Themthu to his son, but it was not permitted to teach him in isolation. He has to be accompanied by his sister or mother.[61] So in that way women learnt themthu though it was not the intention of the priest.

It was also reported that Mrs. Deikho from Gampal village, Ukhrul District, Manipur also functioned as priestess. She is still alive.[62]

Mrs. Lunglhing Kipgen, wife of Keijakai in Thingbong village of Burma also performed the function of the priest (Thempu).[63]

Therefore, a close look into the society shows that Kuki women took part along with men in most of the religious festivals and ceremonies, for example, Lomkivah (festival of members of the Lom youth corps of the village); Hun (feast connected with crops and others); Anthah lop (feast connected with first fruits), Hun (religious Ceremony) etc.

Among the known ceremonies 'Chang-ai' is the only ceremony performed by women and it is also for woman. 'Chang' means paddy and 'ai' means victory. So Chang-ai means victory over paddy. The Kukis believed that the housewife is the owner of paddy when a woman or a family has collected a large amount of grain and has a surplus that family may celebrate chang-ai at the end of the year with a great feast. A particular date for the day of celebration is fixed in consultation with the village priest. The woman who performs this ritual has to feed the whole village for one day and a platform is erected up on the ground about six inches high bordered with small stones within this border are placed. More smaller stones which represent the number of Bengs (women's basket) of rice which is being consumed on that day.[64] A woman who performed the Chang-ai is also honoured with a special memorial stone of about three feet high in front of which are placed three others supporting a flat stone. A space about four square yards in front is enclosed, by a line of stones set on edge, the whole of the interior being planted with small stones which are supposed to show the number of baskets of paddy reaped on the occasion of the Ai.[65] The purpose of 'Chang-ai' is to guarantee a good place in Mithikho (abode of the death) by the performer. The woman of the house is honoured by giving permission to wear the hand woven traditional shawl known as Thangnang.

It is interesting to note that Kuki women played a leading part in the very unique and important cultural feast called Chang-ai. Here the feast is conducted under the sole supervision and direction of the women. Here again the Kuki women takes the role of decision maker.

(VI) KUKI WOMEN'S ROLE IN THE CHURCH

The Kukis received Christianity in the early part of the second decade of the 20th century.[66] Christianity came to the Kukis as a dynamic force in the face of strong opposition from the village chiefs and priests. Those who were converted to Christianity were persecuted by the village Chiefs and priests. But intervention coming from the government and the missionaries restrained them from further persecution. The world of the village priest was fast-shrinking around him and he stood alone as a helpless spectator.

J. Roy contended that "Christianity as it has been preached by the European and American missionaries has succeeded in modernizing the tribal people of Manipur. Indeed it has unlocked and opened up the closed doors of those primitive villages to the light of the modern world. In promoting the modern education, referring the social ills and curing diseases, the helping hand of those philanthropic missions are always there. Christianity has not only brought these hill-men from darkness to light but also has earned for them prestige and regard from others which they never had before."[67]

Christianity gave a new world view through the message of the Gospel. When a Kuki became a Christian the indoi/ Doibom (house deity) was removed from the house by the Pastor and his assistants and destroyed.

All the observances of special days, festivals, taboos in the society were all given up. In the pre-Christian period every feast and ceremony was followed by excessive drinking of Ju (rice beer). Missionaries introduced a substitute and Ju is replaced by tea. Since the traditional songs and dances have been stopped, the new generation of Kukis hardly knows traditional songs and dances which forms a very vital part of community living in Kuki culture. But family relationships, Kinship and customs associated with Tucha, Becha, Naopui Inlut are still practiced today.

The Haosa (Chief) still functions in every Kuki village though the Haosa does not enjoy similar privileges of the traditional Kuki village. The council of elders or Semang-Pachong still exists and they exercise the laws of inheritance, etc and the lands are administered according to the primitive Kuki customs. This council still continues to function in the Christian community.

Christianity has brought a new style of life to the Kukis. The establishment of the Church soon brought about a sense of unity and solidarity among the Kukis. Christianity created a consciousness about their political identity and this has brought together not only the members of one tribe, but also members of different neighbouring tribes under a common platform called Kuki-Inpi. Christianity also help the tribals with the process of modernization. Therefore, the influence of the missionaries was very great especially on the Kukis who attended the mission schools. Literature too played an important role in creating a new tribal culture. The Kuki language became a written language for the first time when the late Mr. Ngulhao published the first Kuki Primer in 1927. The first Kuki New Testament was published in 1944. Modern civilization has come to the Kukis and many have believed Christianity to be a way of civilized means.

Though nothing much about the activities of women in the early Christianity were recorded, it is to be noted that women were found equally in number among the first baptized Christians along with the men. In 1940, women like Nengkholhai Chanloukim, Lamjakim, Nengkhochin and Phatinlhing preached the Gospel in the non-Christian villages in Assam. After the formation of Kuki Christian Church (KCC) in Asam, Nengthai, Lalkhongah, Suali, Kholnei and Ngahpi were appointed as "Bible women" in 1970s. They were involved in preaching and teaching roles. However this post of "Bible women" was abolished in the Kuki Christian Church in 1981.[68]

The Kuki Church organizations as a whole has separate fellowship for women, the women society department. This is the only area in the church where Kuki women exercise leading roles.

All the women fellowship have different means of raising funds through which they contribute much to the Church. One of their main incomes is 'Khutsip Anchang' or handful of rice. In Mizo it is called 'Buhfai Tham'. Women put aside uncooked rice, with the idea that this small amount of rice would not make difference in the meal from the amount which they were going to cook. They set aside the rice in a container and later collected in to be sold. This handful of rice project has become a big fund raising project, in the church. 'Gamthim Thing Kheh' or Missionary fire-wood is also another way of fund raising project for the Kuki women. Women collect firewood from the surrounding forests. Every time they collect the firewood they set aside one piece at Khomol (outskirt gate of the village) and when they meet for their fellowship they take with them one piece each to the church. And later they are auctioned. The money is used for missionary work. Other sources are such as jumble sales, weaving of clothes, working in other's fields for daily wages, talent money, fasting prayer rice (when women have fasting prayer they gathered their share of meal and sold it. The money is used for missionary work and kept as their fund.)

These are some of the sources of income through which they contributed to the Church. Most women fellowship take initiative in helping the poor and the needy. They visit the homes of those in need or sick, or in the hospitals, prisons, orphanages, rehabilitation centres or bereaved families etc. They also felicitate those who have achieved success in studies or career. It is always the women who take initiative part in organising Bible camp for youth, widows, couples children and women and sometimes for their husbands.

Women also go for preaching tour which is called 'Gambih' tour (area tour to visit the women fellowship in pastorate areas). The main purpose is to encourage the 'Gambih' women spiritually and to collect the fund which they have to pay to the office. Most of the leaders are lay women, housewives busy with their household responsibilities. However, despite all these difficulties they could always fulfill their responsibilities succeesfully.[69] Therefore, Kuki women's role in the church is an active one and they are the backbone of the Kuki Church.

We have seen Kuki women's contribution and activities in the church administration. However, their participation in leadership role as well as in decision making body seems to be very minimal. Almost all Kuki women are Christians and regular church goers and yet the church does not allow women positions of authority. Their roles seem to be confined only in secondary roles of assistance. Because none of the Kuki churches has women Head Deacon, Secretary Pastor etc.

Moreover, women who have followed their husbands' ministries have often denied themselves their own gifts and contributions or have offered it quietly with no fanfare or public recognition. There are women who have worked diligently not only with rural and urban poor women but also with women in theology with little acknowledgement of their contribution. One might conceive that - the church, which preaches equality often, promotes this discrimination and gender bias. Christian families also follow these norms which patriarchy has set in society. The struggle for equality of women and men within the church will not take root unless it is linked with the wider struggle for empowerment in society. Efforts to bring about equal participation of women within the church received its impetus from the secular women's movement. Despite the presence of many Christian women within the secular movement for change, the very same women have not been able to affect the church in a significant way. The Church is in fact far behind the state in granting privileges to women and use scriptural arguments to deny women their rightful place.

Many churches today ordain women and allow women to be represented within the decision making bodies of the church and yet the attitude of most men towards women is far from the ideal. There is still a great amount of suspicion and possible fear that hinders the church from giving women their rightful place in the church.[70]

R.B. Edwards rightly pointed but that caring, nurturing and other pastoral function if the clergy are precisely the kind of activities which outside the church are regularly associated with women.[71] Though women seem to possess more pastoral qualities than men the church, however, does not open for broader aspects of women's ministry particularly in pastoral ministry. Therefore, till today, with the exception of Kuki Baptist Convention(K.B.C.) none of the association of the Kuki churches allow women's ordination and pastoral ministry. For the first time, Kuki Baptist Convention became the first in Manipur and the second church organization in N.E.I. to ordain a woman. She was Miss Nemneikim Vaiphei ordained in 1998.[72] The first one is Ao Baptist Church Association of Nagaland.

The fact that ordination was done with the condition that a lady ordained should not get married. Therefore, when Rev. Kim Vaiphei got married in February, 2003, there were many oppositions and strong criticisms particularly from male leaders of the Church. Hence, it may not be wrong to say that the concept of women ordination with an imposition of single life is rather discrimination against women than empowerment. Therefore, one can see that even theologically trained leaders have in adequate knowledge of empowering women as they emphasize that ordained women should not get married. It is a fact, that Christianity and modernization and the western culture accompanying it have not obliterated the ethnicity of the Kuki tribe. A pastor has not replaced Thempu (Priest) who leads all religious ceremonies, whom the animistic Kuki community could not do without. In contrast, the pastor in the modern society plays a minimal role, by leading in prayer the assembled audience or delivering a brief sermon on the basic moral and Christian ethics.

As the Kuki society is now being a Christian society, religion plays an important role in enhancing the status of the women. The contribution of Christianity towards upliftment of women has been tremendous. In spite of the amount of suspicion and possible fear that hinders the Church from giving women empowerment in the church, women are allowed to do all she can within her capacity in the church ministry. Thankfully, the church on its part is slowly promoting the welfare and status of women which were not given much importance because of the strong age-old traditional concept that women are inferior to man. The church being a fellowship of believers consisting of men and women, high and low, rich and poor must be based on the teachings of Jesus Christ who made no discrimination of sexes.

We have seen that Kuki women are capable of holding leadership position and it would be advocated that it is the duty of the church to include them in decision making body and not just as representatives of the whole congregation. The Kuki churches must follow the example. Pastor David Younggi Cho of South Korea included women in his ministry. He says,[73] "for five thousand years in Korea, women had no voice at all. They were only to cater to the need of men. Then Christianity came and set women free. Especially in the church, women are free in Korea. In ministry they are equal with men. They are licensed; they are ordained and they become cell leaders. Out of fifty thousand cell leaders in my church, forty seven thousand are women. I have about six hundred associate pastors; four hundred of them are women. They are wonderful workers.

Without women I don't think I could have built this big Church by empowering women we are evangelizing all of Korea." Thus by appointing women Pastor Cho produced the world's largest church in Korea. In the same way if the Kuki Churches give support, encourage and gives equal importance with men, Kuki women will certainly help in the progress and growth of the church.

In conclusion, I would like to point out that Christianity certainly has brought about modernization and irreversible changes for the Kukis, their search for identity continues whether it be in politics, in the church or in the greater community. The coming out of different denominations in the Kuki Churches resulted in separation and further search for identity in the new found religion. The Kuki society with the onset of modernization is experiencing a sudden break between tradition and modernity. This resulted in social unrest. Having lost the culture of dignity of labour many young people are involved in extortion, drug culture, drunkenness, immorality dishonesty in work, prostitution and many young people are in search of employment. Moreover, the spirit of gun culture is so pervasive that it hinders the peaceful co-existence among the people. Kuki women, with the coming of Christianity and after getting adjustment with the changing society and with the increase in number of educated Kuki women, started to take part in movements for the development of the Kuki society. Therefore, Kuki women should be encouraged to take full participation in social life, political activities and in the church.

Far more needs to be done in the area of reinterpreting the Bible from the feminist perspective and affecting the manner in which the church addresses the many social evils that confront women in everyday life. The Church should be willing to encourage women's participation much more than before because in every congregation there are more women than men. This perhaps would put an end to many of the political struggles and divisions in the churches which in turn affects the society at all levels.

It is quite evident that for years Kuki women have displayed enormous sense of dedication, devotion and adherence towards their family, faith and community.

Historically and culturally speaking the society in which they do well remain by and large patriarchal in which male members have been traditionally assigned 'masculine' roles in the public arena and their female counterparts customarily expected to embody female characteristics by taking pride in running errands within the private/domestic spheres. But there appears to have seemingly been gender inversion, that is, the reversal or circulation of gender specific roles in current times.

It is also worthy to note that the inherited primitive beliefs in sanctioning outmoded gender roles fostered and substantiated by the passive and non-resistant image of leading role models in the Bible such as the Virgin Mary. Christianity and its precepts play an influential role in determining the ways of the Kuki society and the duties befitting each individual.

This is one of the many results of British colonization and the widespread of Christian religion to the indigenous tribe by way faring missionaries. Christianity has worked both for and against the community in that, on the one hand it gives women emancipation and gave them the freedom to realize their dreams and talents and service. On the other hand, it also teaches the men to appreciate their mothers, sisters and wives and give them their due respect, thereby maintaining gender balance as such. Also, one must not forget that we are looking at a typically agrarian society with primordial ways of living and thinking. A lot of people view their indigenous way of life as unique and morally relevant to them. The values that are considered naïve and crude from western or comparatively modern perspective may ostensibly be considered a cherished attribute by the Kuki women, a quality which is peculiar and distinguishing of their culture, people and society. Thus, Gangte concludes, that "the situation developed and fresh mental make up started growing to buttress the entire changing processes while absorbing them in their strides or better civilization".[74]

References

1. J. Shakespear, The Lushai Kuki Clans (1912); p. 147.
2. Journal of the 69th Anniversary of the Kuki Rebellion, 1917-19; 1985; p. 10.
3. G.A. Grierson; The Linguistic Survey of India, Vol. 3, Part II & III.
4. Bertram S. Carey and H.N. Tuck: The Chin Hills; Calcutta, Firma KLM Pvt. Ltd., 1976; p. 135.
5. Tualchin Neihsial, History and Culture of Zomis; [Ph.D. Thesis (Unpublished) M.U. Department of History], 1993; p. 12.
6. K. Kipgen, The Thadou Kukis; p. 3.
7. Khamkam G., Manipur Past and Present, Vol. 3, edited by Naorem Sanajaoba, Mittal Publication, New Delhi, p. 297.
8. Gangte, T.S., The Kukis of Manipur – A Historical Analysis; Gyan Publishing House, New Delhi; p. 26.
9. Goswami Tarun; Kuki life and lore, North Cachar Hill District, Haflong, Assam (1985); p. 19.
10. Ibid., Gangte; p. 95.
11. Longman is a customary duty consisting of one mithun, claimable by the maternal uncle of the heir on the death of his nephew and their mother. It is paid by the father or the eldest son. However, Longman can not be claimed in the case of unnatural death and women who bear no male issues.
12. Tyson Lois : Critical Theory Today, Second Edition, Routledge, 2006, New York.
13. T.S. Gangte : The Kukis of Manipur, 1993; pp. 125-126.
14. Goswami Tarun : Kuki Life and Lore, published by North Cachar Hills District Council, Haflong, Assam, 1985; p. 87.

15. Col. J. Shakespear : Lushai Kuki Clans, 1912; p. 42.
16. Statistical Account of Bengal : D.K. Publishing House, Delhi (Reprint), 1973, Vol. VI; p. 60.
17. Chatterjee. N., The Mizo Chief and His Administration,1975; pp. 3-4.
18. Thangtindal : Ancient Polity of the Gangtes, 1988; p. 2.
19. Verrier Elvin, Democracy in NEFA, Shillong, 1965; p.15.
20. Personal Interview : Dr.(Mrs.) M. Priyadarshni Gangte, on 10th April, 2007.
21. Reported by Paokhohen Haokip, Chief of Sita Village, Chandel District, Manipur.
22. Nemjating Gangte is the sister-in-law of the writer.
23. Interview : Mrs. Ating Haokip (Chief of Saivom Village in Chandel District of Manipur) on 27th May, 2007.
24. Personal interview of Mrs. Lhingjaneng Gangte, Member, Manipur State Commission for Women.
25. Personal interview with Miss Kim Gangte, Ex-M.P.(Outer Manipur) on 12 June 2006 at Langol.
26. Dr. T. Lunkim: Kuki Inpi (Kuki Government), Published by the Author.
27. Jamkithang Sitlhou, Thadou Puchon Pachon, p. 49.
28. S.Kipgen: Political and Economic History of the Kukis of Manipur (Ph.D. Thesis submitted to M.U.), p. 158.
29. E.W. Dun: A Bridged Gazetteer of Manipur, Simla – 1891, Vivek Publishing House, Delhi, 1975; pp. 32-35.
30. Foreign and Political Department, 27th June-8th July, 1919.
31. Lal Dena, British Policy towards Manipur (1891-1991), Churachandpur L&R Printing Press, 1984.
32. Report of Webster, Secretary to the Chief Commissioner of Assam to the Secretary, Government of India.
33. Government of India's letter No.4326-1-A dated 1st Oct., 1919.
34. Report of Webster, For & Poll Dept, 1919.
35. Secretary to the Governor of Assam's letter No.93 dated 22nd April, 1919 to the Govt. of India.
36. Manipur Praja Sanmelani Amasung Anisuba Nupi Lan by Laikhuram Ibobi Singh, 2003; p. 123.

37. Quoted in Souvenir – Golden Jubilee Celebration of the AZAD HIND GOVERNMENT – 21 Oct., 1993, Moirang, p. 68.
38. Administrative Report of Manipur State for the year 1892-93; p. 8.
39. Vumson; Zo History, Aizawl, 1986; p. 64.
40. K. Kipgen, Op. Cit, p. 114.
41. T.S. Gangte; Seminar Paper, MUTSU, 2001; p. 2.
42. Sanajaoba : Manipur, Vol. 3, p. 155.
43. Sina Khayi; "Cultural Significance of tribal Costumes in Modern Times" – Seminar paper presented to MUTSU, March, 1996,
44. Pudaite Rochunga : The Education of Hmar People, Sielmat, Churachandpur, 1963; pp. 51-52.
45. Hudson : The Naga tribes of Manipur; B.R. Publishing Corporation, 461, Vivekanand Nagar, Delhi: Reprint 1974; p. 61.
46. Manipur Administrative Report, 1919-20.
47. Manipur Administrative Report, 1913-14.
48. Political Agent : Tour Diary No.10th Feb., 1986 (State Archives).
49. Personal interview with Mrs. Rose Mangshi, retired Lecturer of G.P. Women's College, Imphal.
50. Personal interview with Mrs. Chingthem Kipgen, IAS (Commissioner, SCERT, Government of Manipur.).
51. D. Singson: The Kuki Christian Church of India; (unpublished) D.Min. Thesis; Evengelical Divinity School Deerfield, Illinois, 1985; p. 50.
52. Singson, D: The Kuki Christian Church of India (Thesis submitted for degree of Missiology), 1985; p. 20.
53. William Shaw : Notes on Thadou Kukis ; p. 75.
54. Thangkim Haolai, Kuki Culture in North Cachar Hills – Before and After The Advent of Christianity; p. 54.
55. Gangte T.S.; The Kukis of Manipur; 1993, p. 194.
56. Shingkhawkai: Zo People And Their Culture, 1995 ; p. 176.
57. Goswami, 1985; p. 178.
58. Kipgen : The Thadou Kukis; A brief Account of History and Culture, p. 119.

59. N.M. Changsan: "The Prophetic Role of Women in OT And Its Significance for The Kuki Women in The New Millennium"; B.D. Thesis ETC Jorhat, 1997; p. 16.
60. Tinkholhing Haokip : The Status and Role of Kuki Women in the Church and Society, (B.D. Thesis ETC Jorhat, 1994; p. 27).
61. Interviewed Rev. Seikholet Singson on 30th April, 2003 at Bongmoul Village, Manipur.
62. Reported by P.T. Jamthang, a social worker, now he is no more.
63. Personal interview of Mrs. Hoikhovei Kipgen, (daughter of late Lungthing Kipgen) at Old Lambulane, Imphal.
64. Shaw, William : The Thadou Kuki; Cultural Publishing House, New Delhi, 1929; p. 74.
65. Shakespear, J.: The Lushei Kuki Clan, 1912; p. 205.
66. Primer, S. Vaiphei : Church growth among the hill tribes in Manipur, North East India Imphal (Heneng Vaiphei, 1986 ; 47).
67. Jyotirmoy Roy : History of Manipur, Calcutta : Loyal Art Press, 1973; p. 200.
68. Henkhovum Haolai : A Historical study of the Development of Christianity among the Kukis of North Cachar Hills District of Assam with special reference to Kuki Christian Church Synod and its missiological implication, 1971; p. 106.
69. Kipgen Tingneilhing : The Leadership Role of Women in Fourth Gospel in The Eyes of Kuki Women in Manipur, 2004; p. 78.
70. Personal Interview of Rev. Paokhosei Kipgen, Hengbung Village, Senapati District, Imphal.
71. Ruth. B. Edwards : The Case for Women's Ministry (London S.P.C.K, 1989); p. 163.
72. Personal Interview of Mrs. Nemneikim Vaiphei, Pastor, K.B.C. Chassad Avenue.
73. Source obtained from Internet : David Younggi Cho, "Don't Be Afraid to empower women" a sermon preached in February, 1999 at Crowns of Beauty Conference in Italy.
74. Gangte, Ibid, 1993; pp. 225-226.

5

Naga Women's Role

(I) NAGA WOMEN'S ROLE IN SOCIETY

The origin of the word 'Naga' itself is shrouded in mystery. Captain John Butler, who was then the new Principal Assistant Commissioner at Nowgong is also of the opinion that the tribes now living in Nagaland had no generic term applicable to the whole race. He further asserts that the tribal folk preferred to use a specific name for a group of villages.[1] When asked they would merely say that they belonged to such and such-village; they were quite ignorant of any distinctive tribal name connecting them to any particular group of villages.[2]

The Naga areas in Manipur measure 15,519 sq. Km.[3] The hill tribes of Manipur though divided into innumerable clans and sections may be considered generally under the two great divisions of Kuki and Naga. The Nagas are scattered over the hill districts of Manipur but chiefly to the west, North and North-east.[4]

Differences of stature, dress, coiffure and weapons make it easy to distinguish between the members of these tribes. In colour they are all brown with but little variety, though some of the Tangkhuls who earn their living by selling salt-making seem to be darker. Among them all, as among the Manipuris there are persons who have a tinge of colour in their cheeks when still young.[5]

Nagas are one of the indigenous tribes of the North East India. Nagas who inhabits the extreme eastern part of India form a living and vibrating culture with great values of life. It is very difficult to give a general account of the many tribes covered by the word "Naga" for there are both differences and similarities among them just as there are many aspects of their life and culture which can be paralleled by tribes in other parts of India. The Nagas according to R.R. Shimray "are stalwart athletic and of medium size with broad shoulder and high cheek bones. Their colour is like that of the Burmese, the Indonesians, the Malaysians, the Thais, the Japanese and the Chinese".[6]

The secrets and the charms of these highlanders lie in their community life which is so scarce and so unique and their community life so colourful with their culture. They have rich culture and traditions and their beautiful arts and crafts speak undoubtedly of their rich culture and tradition which stood the test of time and also reflects the cultures of the society.

Das writes "Generally the Naga tribes live in compact big sized villages in east, north, and west districts of Manipur."[7]

According to Gangmumei Kabui, the Rongmei had settled down in Imphal valley since the eighteenth century and in the Cachar District of Assam.[8]

It is found that the Mao, Paomei, Maram and Thangal inhabit the northern parts of Manipur Hills which has now came to be known as Senapati District. The Tangkhul another populous Naga tribe occupy the North Eastern Hills of Ukhrul

District. They were one of the powerful tribes of the hills as far as the Chindwind.[9]

Naga society as found in its villages was a well knit society where rigid customs and discipline were observed. As the village was an independent unit, customary laws were supreme and dispensation of punishment was very fast and quick. The Nagas once settled in a place were almost glued to it and rarely moved out to a new place from cradle to grave and identified himself with his village. In order to understand the Naga women and their roles in society, we have to peep into time and space as social changes occur at all levels and at various times among the Naga tribes.

In Naga society, family is the basic social institution. Naga society is also both patriarchal and patrilineal and thus descent is traced from father's side. This proved that women are not equal to men in status concerning certain aspects. Women are considered physically weaker than men which is the reason why the Naga men feel responsible towards women.

As a daughter, wife and mother Naga women play a significant role. They are given full authority regarding the domestic affairs. Men keep themselves away from the domestic affairs since they consider it below their dignity to indulge in such activities. In traditional Naga society, normally the daughters are very close to their parents, especially to the mothers. Amother plays an important role in the family as she performs all household chores apart from growing vegetables, educating her children the art of weaving and handicrafts. She also helps her husband and is the real partner of her husband. She is very hardworking and accompanies her husband everywhere except in hunting.

Inequality between men and women is linked to a complex historical process and is manifested in ways and varied as social and cultural conditions of the community.[10]

Women whether literate or illiterate and employed or unemployed, were found to perform similar roles and duties where domestic work was concerned. According to Mills "They weave the clothing required for the family, work in the fields, cut and bring in firewood and perform all manners of drudgery".[11]

J. Johnstone says "The Naga women are not handsome but very pleasant looking, and many of the girls are pretty, but soon age with the hard toil they have to perform working in the fields and carrying heavy loads up endless hills. They have plenty of spirit and can generally hold their own .... Their women weave substantial and pretty coloured cloths".[12]

As can be seen, women take for granted that a particular set of jobs were solely meant for them and they do not try to change things for the better even though, some times things are a disadvantage to them.

In Naga society a woman has no share in landed properties of her father and of her husband except otherwise acquired by her husband after her marriage with him. The Naga society is so stringent in following the patrilineal system that women are not permitted to have a share in the property even in the absence of a son. In such cases property goes to the nearest male clan of her father's clan.

Widow re-marriage is not prohibited, however if she chooses to remain in her late husband's house to look after their children no restriction is imposed. Polygamy is unknown in the Naga society.

According to Hudson "The women are all much shorter than the men, but strongly built with a muscular development of which the men would not be ashamed. Before aged by the cares and troubles of motherhood and matrimony, they are often comely, with handsome figures. The habit of suckling children until they are four years of age or even more soon destroys the soft fullness of the bosom and women of thirty are to all appearance aged hags worn and wrinkled".[13]

They are industrious but the unpleasant task which make up the daily round all fell to the women, who take at least their fair share in the work of cultivation. Due to the hard working she takes no further care about her personal appearance.

It is true that as a wife, Naga women have considerable freedom to take important decisions about any family matters in the absence of male family members. In her husband's home also she occupies a high position and her children treated her well. Among the Maram and Tangkhul Naga Tribes "Ava Pamkhong" meaning Mother's seat ort throne was given only to the mother. No one could trespass on the seat of the mother. She enjoys a high place in the family. "If the grain falls short due to mismanagement of the domestic affair, the accusing finger points to her disapprovingly not only she should be and example by her hard work but she must also learn to extract work from her children".[14]

"Equal status should be given to both male and female. Individual potentiality should be recognised and women must be given space to use her talent".[15]

Naga women enjoy the same status as the men and suffer no discrimination on account of sex. Widows are allowed to remarry without any stigma. Being a classless society, Naga women enjoy rights and privileges guaranteed under the Naga customary laws of their respective tribes.[16]

About the social status of Naga women, Haimendorf writes thus "Many women in more civilized parts of India may well envy the women of Naga Hills, their high status and their happy life; and if you measure the cultural level of people by the social position and personal freedom of its women you will think twice before looking down the Nagas as savages".[17]

In the Nagas' society "there was no dowry system, no sati, no purdah system, no child marriage no bride burning, no female child infanticide."[18] Bride price is also paid by the bridegroom to the bride's family. This system is called *Chaman lubo* in Zeliangrong Naga. Divorce was rare among the Nagas but sometimes this led to many unpleasant wars between the villages. Divorce system also varies from tribe to tribe among the Nagas. A girl could be divorced on grounds of barrenness, personal incompatibility differences and infidelity. In many cases divorce was settled by the relatives of the husband and the wife without resorting to litigation. Sometimes a woman could be divorced by returning the bride price.

"Women are prohibited from having any say in both social and family affairs in the Zeliangrong Naga society because they believe that the presence of women in such affairs is a bad omen for the whole society. It is tabooed for a warrior to sleep with his wife or even touch her inner clothes before going to war or for hunting."[19]

This shows that women are considered as subordinate to men in Zeliangrong Naga society. Traditionally, women were free from danger and physical tortures during the time of inter village feuds.

Torturing and killing of children and women were considered to be an act of cowardice. In order to avoid harm to the women and children the Naga warriors would always give a warning yell before they attack the village of their enemy.

During inter village wars Naga woman acts like an ambassador. She is granted special power to stop the interline wars through negotiations or to intervene the war directly. For her security, a special act was enacted which forbids any man to lay a hand on her. She enjoyed full diplomatic immunity.

"She was called the peace maker, the bearer of torch of peace and the Red Cross bearer of Naga inter-village war."[20]

She was called Pukhareila (Neutral Lady) in Tangkhul. This neutral lady can physically enter into the midst of the battlefield holding her Zeithing (Y. shaped stick) when negotiations failed. She also tries to prevent the winner side from chasing the defeated party. Many bloody wars were stopped through her interventions. Even in the war of challenges (Ngasungrai in Tangkhul) where only two warriors fight the Pukhareila can intervene at an appropriate stage.

The word "Pukhareila" in Tangkhul means a woman married to a man belonging to a clan other than her own or different village or also a different tribe for that matter.

After the intervention of the Pukhareila neither side would have the courage to raise the weapon against the other. If any one of the warriors disobeyed the command of the Pukhareila and raised his weapon (dao or spear) even if he did not harm anybody, he was considered as an outcast, a disobedient black sheep, a social evil and he received the wrath of all the members of both the warring groups who attacked him. Even if he was killed in this attack, nobody was to be blamed but him. Thus, when there was no daring soul it was the Pukhareila who with all the power and authority in her own right would bring the ugly situation to an end and usher in peace among the warring groups. She was the one who would bridge the gap between the two groups – clans/villages for it was she who had a say on the members of both the sides.

Among the Mao, Paomei and Maram Naga women joined in the war by standing behind the two warring groups. When the fighting became too severe the women of the respective parties would move forward and stop the fighting. The Naga customary laws forbid harming women of both the parties and therefore once the women of both parties made a declaration of peace the warriors should comply and stop the fighting at once. This indeed is a unique custom of the Nagas where women were empowered to intervene and stop the battles.

There are examples where women took the lead in social movement and politics also. The story of the Naga Rani called "Rani Gaidinliu is found in many pages of the History of Independence India. There are others also who are involved in social reforms and social services.[21]

In the traditional Naga society boys and girls after the attainment of puberty, lived in their respective youth chambers (Morungs) till they were married. It is called NGALALONG in Tangkhul; Louchizii Fii in Paomei; Raliiki in Maram; Lochii in Mao; 'Khangchiu' for boys and 'Liuchiu' or 'Kailiu' for girls in Rongmei. Among the Naga tribes, "the Zeliangrongs do not have separate house for dormitories but they are attached to one well to do family, so that the husband and wife of the house may play the role of advisorship".[22]

"Here, in the dormitory, young girls learned many more things about social behaviour, manner and obedience[23] from seniors and it is here that, for the girls, the way was paved for her futures responsibility as a mother. It shaped and built the moral character and taught them social responsibility.

She would leave the 'morung' only when she is married, betrothed, or lost her virginity. Girls are also taught singing, dancing, weaving, handicrafts, discipline etc in the Morung. R.R. Shimray remarks that it was in the dormitories that one could forget his personal worries and problems.

In social activities Naga women are allowed to participate except in war dance and head taking victory celebration.

Social stability and harmony of the Nagas is enhanced by their hardworking women. Through their hard-work, patience, sincerity and morally upright life women instill the intrinsic values of Naga life to their children. It is also she who goads on her husband and children to participate in all social and economic activities such as cultivation, games and sports, singing, dancing, house construction, dormitory life, community working, festivities etc.

Though woman occupies prominent position within the family and the society, certain restrictions are imposed on her. It was forbidden for women to step over men. If a woman stepped over a man, the man becomes an accursed one. It was therefore, restricted to women to step over men. Women cannot become a priest; women cannot wear Haora/Luirim i.e. male shawls.[24]

Women cannot sit cross legged and she cannot put her leg on men. Women should not touch the spear and shield of man for those are the weapons of battle. It is considered that the sanctity and efficiency of the weapons are lost the moment she touches the weapons. Women cannot join hunting party and they cannot loosen their hair before the village elders. It is also "tabooed for a warrior to sleep with his wife or even touch her inner clothes before going to war or for hunting". Because the Nagas believed that this action would bring about undesirable consequences to the whole group of warriors of which he is a member.

Wrestling is held every year during the transplantation (paddy) festival and other festivals. A circular line is drawn around the field of wrestling in which no woman is allowed to enter. During the wrestling no woman is allowed to comment anything whatsoever.

Women are considered a spy of the enemy. During the time of war it is forbidden to leak any sort of strategy of the village to any woman for the fear of becoming spy of the enemies. Women are compared with summer rain. Summer rain comes without thunder, goes and hides in the midst of the cloud. No one knows when it will rain. Women are considered solely responsible for quarrel within the clansmen and neighbours.

All these show that women are considered subordinate to men in Naga society. Inspite of the many restrictions imposed on women, Naga women have been a source of inspiration not only in the domestic front but also in the society at large. Naga women formed a vital part of the Naga society.

(II) NAGA WOMEN'S ROLE IN POLITICS

Political participation of women in the decision making body has been a taboo for women traditionally and it continued even today particularly in the villages. The village council is the apex political body of the Naga Community. Each Naga village forming a republic affords the citizens to participate in every decision making directly or through their representatives who are elected in the best possible democratic manner through casting of hands or voice votes. All decisions being taken on consensus through the participation of every member and hence warmly personal with strong and vibrant sense of belonging in community life, no one fell alienated. In the administration of justice too, no problem or case is too difficult to solve in by the wisdom of the village elders (village council members). They administer justice openly, justly and efficiently that no one dare to defy the village or in the administration of justice there is nothing which denies women's participation.

"In politics and diplomacy women could influence in many ways directly or indirectly through the village Councillors or at least through their husband or their father. As neutral lady, she had the right of her own to intervene in the war and if she had prior approval of her husband, a warrior or village council, she might strike a balance in the war."[25]

In villages where efficient male leadership is not available women take the leadership.

There were instances where women took lead in politics among the Nagas of Manipur, for instance Mrs. Hinga

Karangnamei continues to exercise power of Sagungpui (Chieftainship) of Maram Khullen, Senapati District, Manipur after the demise of her husband. She is the chief of 23 clans of the Maram tribe. Similar cases are found in the Mayon and Tangkhul tribes etc.

Among the Tangkhuls one exceptional lady called Harkhongla of Maram village was elected to the village Council. She led the warriors of her village in war as the commander in chief. So complete was her domination over her people that the villagers submitted themselves willingly to her leadership in politics, diplomacy and war.

Another woman called Kaireila of Talui also preceded the Council sitting and joined the discussions. Besides them there are others like "Shakhala of Mangchon, Seikhangla of Laotei, Lamengla of Tuinem were renowned women of Tangkhul hills in the field of politics."[26]

Among the Zeliangrong community, Rani Gaidinliu from Longkao village in Tamenglong District of Manipur dedicated her life in order to preserve the traditional socio-economic and political structure of the tribe against the British Imperialism. "Rani Gaidinliu fought alone to preserve the culture and to bring back the past glory."[27] At her instance political awareness could widely spread not only among the Zeliangrong women but also among the other women of Manipur.

The political participation among the Kabui Naga women is considerably increasing day by day. Reservation of one third seats for women in the Panchayati Raj institutions and in the urban bodies gave women opportunities to make a space for themselves in the local decision making structures. There are some Kabui Naga women as Councillors in Imphal Municipal bodies and as elected members in some Gram Sabhas. In this modern times, the Kabui Naga women can actively participate in all level of politics. In 1947 Late Mrs. Shiningla Keishing was nominated in the Manipur Territorial Legislative Assembly.[28] Another woman late Mrs. Hangmila Shaiza was popularly elected as member of Manipur Legislative Assembly on Janata Dal ticket from Ukhrul constituency in 1990. Mrs. Grace Shatsang and Mrs. Valley Rose Hungyo also contested in the previous elections but were defeated.

Among the Tangkhul Naga, women have the right to vote in the Lok Sabha State Assembly and District Council elections. But not in the elections of Village Council, Longphang and Tangkhul Long which are the real traditional political institutions. Woman does not enjoy the same right as the man in her own society. She is not included in the traditional political decision making. A woman Headman is unknown. But women do come to the village council whenever they have cases to put up and also do give witnesses for or against any case in the village court/Council.

"Finding lack of women's participation in the village council and important public meetings the youth of Sirarakhong village, Ukhrul District, Manipur made it a right to include women in all decision making bodies through a resolution. Women of Tungjoy village, Senapati District, Manipur enjoy rights to be invited to and consulted in the village council important issues like social, political, cultural and economic matters. Even as there is no women representatives in the village council in the discussion of matters relating to a woman, women are to be consulted by the village council. Similarly the same tradition is practised in the Naga Church administration. Apart from all these undertakings and participations the advice of women is sought in crucial situation.[29]

In the Naga society, the two factors which acted as catalyst in the process for the right and equality of women are the Naga political movement and the violation of Human Rights against women by the armed forces in the name of counter insurgency. "The leaders of the Naga Nationalists call for every Naga man and woman to join hands in their capacity to work for national rights and freedom, to set up Nagaland for Christ, many women joined the movement as soldiers, nurses, teachers and so on."[30] Again the humiliating treatment of the armed forces towards Naga women gave them a sense to organize themselves to fight and to protect their rights. These gave the Naga women a new sense of political participation among the Naga women. Women have begun to raise their voices against social evils and against the oppression especially in urban areas.

Due to lack of awareness women in rural areas did not fully participate in the political and social movements. Having strongly felt that woman needs to be organized to achieve growth, women in every tribe formed societies or associations to solve the problems facing the Naga society as a whole.

These associations are formed under the umbrella of Naga women's Union, Manipur. The Naga women union is the apex organisation of all the Manipur State Naga Women. Many women organisations and NGO's worked actively in various social activities and issues. Some of the registered women organisations of the tribes are

(1) Anal Sinnu Ruwl;
(2) Lamkang Snu Lop;
(3) Maram Women's Union;
(4) Mao Naga Women Welfare Association;
(5) Paumai Naga Women Organisation;
(6) Tangkhul Sanao Long;
(7) Thangal Women's Union;
(8) Zeliangrong Women Society (Zeliangrong Taupui), etc.

"Naga women have always taken an active part in their people's struggle to maintain or protect their rights to self determination and against social evils in the society."[31]

In example, as mentioned earlier Queen Pei Hinga who ruled Maram Khullen since 1965 till today is well known for her justice. Many social changes has been introduced by her in the Maram society. M-bong Katai – which means death in childbirth, is one of the evil practices of the Maram in the olden days. According to this traditional law a pregnant mother who is under hard labour is ill treated. If the mother lost the hope of giving birth, she is taken outside from the house, thinking that to let a pregnant mother die inside the house desecrate the whole house. She is discharged from the room and kept outside along where no one should touch her. Thus, many women and new born babies died due to this evil practice in the society. The villagers do not join for funeral of such kind of death. All the materials of the expired woman is thrown away. This practice, being too cruel for Maram women, was reformed by Pei-Hinga, the present Queen of Maram. She declared this law to be null and void in 1968.

Inter marriage among different Khel or society of Maram Khullen village was not encouraged. This unwanted law was reformed in 1975 by the Queen and declared the right to have inter-marriage among the Marams.

Again, according to the Maram tradition, the King/Queen performs certain rites before plantation takes place. Unless the King plants first, no one is allowed to start plantation in the field. However, this law was reformed by the Queen in 1981 and encourages early plantation.

Thus, "the Queen of Maram Pei-Hinga removed many restrictions imposed on women and helped to eliminate some old, ugly, superstitions that have hampered the female progress."[32] From this example we can come to the conclusion that Naga women are not only capable of contributing their share towards the family economy but are also taking active and leading part in all aspects of Naga life for the over all development of the society. Therefore, when equal opportunities are provided in the decision making bodies of the Naga society women's responsibilities will be more effective and meaningful.

The Naga women of Manipur formed themselves into a union under the title "Naga Women's Union, Manipur (NWUM) on the 7th January, 1994 comprising of all the women of Naga Tribes of the state and became the apex body of all the Women's organisation of the Naga Tribes in Manipur. It stands for the rights and dignity of Naga women.

The Union made an attempt to bring about awareness among the women members themselves of their own positions, responsibilities and instill courage in order to empower them. The Union also works for peace and congenial atmosphere and understanding among different tribes.

On the issue of Human Rights the Union has been carrying out on the spot fact finding investigations with other groups involved in human rights issue. Award scheme was introduced with the objective to motivate girls and women to achieve excellence in academics to outstanding performers. The union also started publication of Magazine name Raisunriang, meaning news link coined out of Naga words, intended to serve as a link in sharing ideas and views on various issues pertaining to Nagas in particular. This was introduced to encourage writing skill among Naga women. One of the major drawbacks of tribal's society is lack of writing and exposure of issues, problems or prospects of the people, whether they are good or bad to the outside world.

The claim of the Union include equal wages for both sexes, for equal amount of work and equal rights to inheritance of properties movable and immovable for both female and male children.

Naga women have been organising themselves in order to raise issues which curtail their rights and raise their voices against oppression. In Manipur East District Women Association was formed in 1974 as a direct response to sexual assaults by B.S.F. men. Among the victim was Miss Rose of Ngaprum Village who committed suicide after being raped."[33]

Being the sustaining force in Naga society the Naga women stand to guard against any force that would attempt to destroy the good culture and customs of the Naga. The Union's intention is to uphold the rights, dignity and equality for women. In 1996 Lok Sabha Election the union issued a Press Release seeking support for women candidates for the cause of women for the first time in the history of Manipur Election. This has created misgiving to some people. But the union's stand was for women's cause not for any individual candidate. Thus, Naga women are fast catching up in the fields of education, profession etc and are sharing many of the privileges hitherto reserved for the menfolk.

Though Christian faith and organized governmental system and modern education introduced in the late 19th century have brought about new perspective and attitude there still exist some age old attitudes in certain oppressive forms.[34]

Some of the oppressive traditional and cultural values which are deep rooted in the minds of the people have for a long time acted and are still acting as tools of oppression. Therefore, the first and foremost work of the Naga women is to find out ways to remove the oppressive mindset of both men and women. Change is possible only when one raises one's voice and is not a mere spectator.

(III) NAGA WOMEN'S ROLE IN ECONOMY

The status of women in the society is intimately connected with its economic position. Naga women are hard working and form childhood, a girl is taught domestic chores. She is expected to get up at dawn, and to do all the household chores. Therefore, a mother in Naga society is happy if she had a baby girl as the first child. With regard to the economic condition of the Naga women, it was not that pathetic and miserable, for women did enjoy a considerable economic right. Dowry is absent in the Naga society but at the time of her marriage her parents can give her property both movable and immovable which become more or less her absolute property. However, ancestral property can not be given to the daughter.

Cultivation is the main occupation among the Naga tribes. Tending livestock like pigs, poultry, cattle, etc are also an indispensable source of income. Therefore, domestic animals play an important part in the economy of the villages. Apart from the management of kitchen and bringing up the children which exert tremendous stress on them they have to look after the rearing and feeding of domestic animals. Mothers on leaving for their work, charged the older daughter, on the first alarm of war, to seize the little one's and flee at once to some hiding place.[35]

The work-field of the Nagas is land and forest, on whose blossom they depend for their livelihood. Agriculture being the mainstay of the economy women's work in the field continue till cropping of grains be it in tilling, sowing, transplanting, weeding or harvesting. Threshing was done by men on huge mats spread on the field and women collected paddy in bundles. Women were entrusted to give the final touch of threshing and winnowing. Both men and women carry paddy in bags then stored in the family granary (Machum in Tangkhul). It is the duty of the women to pound and husk paddy for the family's consumption. Sometimes surplus paddy was sold by barter system in the nearby village. It is also the duty of the women to see that essential varieties of crops and vegetables for their household consumption are grown in their fields or gardens such as ginger, maize, brinjal, garlic, tomato, peas, etc.

Besides, it was their sole responsibility to collect firewood, fetch water from the sources of which are often far off and steep. Income from cash crops was usually considered as family fund although it was managed by the women.

Weaving is also another conspicuous economic activity of the Naga women because weaving industry was considered as a main source of income in traditional Naga society. The art of weaving and dyeing was solely carried out by women. They spin and weave varieties of traditional handloom clothes for the family and also for sale. Handicraft work was done mostly during off-season of cultivation. U.G.Bower writes that "Nowhere have I seen such a concentration of textile as there was in Tuinem village where rolls of blue and crimson cloths were airing outside every house, skeins of dyed thread, red, white, black, orange, green and gold were stretched to dry or lay beside the women as they worked. In every porch was a loom, with a cloth at one stage or another." [36]

Therefore, Naga women were the sustainer and manager of the home. They stand equal to man in every sphere of life and need not entirely depend on their husband's earning.[37]

Sometimes, the woman drudges with her household chores with little help or no help from her husband. With the progress in the field of education more and more women are becoming salaried wives and daughters. The conservative view has slackened giving more scope to girl education. Many women work in unorganized sector or informal sector selling vegetables, firewood, tea, sweets, meat, second hand clothes etc. These are the main sources of income of the Naga women. However, inspite of the increased number of working women, more financial dependence still rest on the men for the majority. The wife's earning is a sort of supplement to the husband's earnings. Improvement of communication helps in the expansion of marketing facility, sources of finance etc and also gave the tribal people the opportunity for wider physical mobility and for the expansion of their economic activities.

Many Nagas, living in Imphal areas have shaken off their traditional pattern of livelihood by taking up different types of occupation.

Today, a woman in salaried job is not looked down upon as crossing the social norms as was the case in yonder days. Grace Satsang, President Naga Women Union is of the opinion that "to keep up with the fast changing society and the increased needs of the family, it is rather encouraged that a woman should do whatever is in her capacity to support and share the family finance".[38]

A recent phenomenon among the tribals is the high priority given to education and the expenditure on schooling incurred by any single family is far out of proportion to its income.

"There are households who are ever at the giving and hardly even at the receiving end, special mention must be made of families living in towns such as Kohima, Dimapur, Makokchung and Imphal, fellow clansmen from the villages often come to these towns to admit their children into schools, to pay their fees, to do their festivals, shopping, to buy goods, to get a bill passed at a particular office, to bail out a detained relative and indeed a hundred such errands, the town based family will be the base for these frequent visitors and will provide boarding lodging, assistance to get about the town and more often than not, the bus fare back to the villages. The ordinary middle class salaried head of such a household does all this at the cost of his own family."[39] This made the family bankrupt on account of such hospitality and greatly affected the family budget as well as the income.

Like everyone else, the Naga society is changing rapidly. Contact with the plains through trade, western education a new religion, "an ordered administration two world wars, the recent disturbances have had varied impact and it does in fact, say much for the vitality of Naga culture that it had not disappeared altogether."[40]

Among the Tangkhuls there are many instances of women possessing landed property, such as, paddy field, woodland, garden etc. The women acquired their property through their own effort. Customary laws of inheritance and possession of immovable property is relaxed in the Naga society to some extent.

"When women can support themselves, have their entry to all the trades and professions, with a house of their own over their heads and a bank account, they will own their bodies and be dictators in the social realm".[41]

Today, there are instances of parents conversion of immovable property into movable property thereby giving the property to their daughter as marriage present. Some parents even gave their wet cultivation field (Laya Lui) to their daughter. Such practice is recognised by the society provided, the property presented is not an ancestry property and their sons "Shim lukat" had no objection to the arrangement. This is a great departure from the traditional custom and practice of the Naga society.

Therefore, it is high time for the patriarchal Naga society to realize that raising the level of skill and the aspirations of women is necessary for Naga society. Women's emancipation in economy is not directed against men, but it aimed at the untapped resources of the society to make the Naga society richer. The social stability and harmony of the Nagas is enhanced by their hardworking women.

(IV) NAGA WOMEN'S ROLE IN RELIGION

Naga people are religious though they do not have the name of their religion. Naga live close to nature and sense its mysterious powers in the belief of the existence of a single supreme God, who was the creation and sustainer of the universe. The concept of the plurality of God (Kameo) was more negative than positive. Fear was certainly the most outstanding characteristic of their religion. Their ordeals, superstitions, belief and taboos were chiefly based on the emotion of fear.[42] They believe that all objects were inhabited by these gods or spirits. When people were in trouble or in fear or in happiness they invoked the gods or Kameo.

Naga religion, which is animistic lay emphasis on the existence and manifestation of spirits, both benevolent and malevolent. Ignorance about nature increased the fear among the Nagas and thus to appease the anger of the deities and gods, sacrifices were made. It is the fear of the wrath of gods which appears to be the primary reason for the sacrifices.

The real religion of the Nagas according to M. Horam was "ancestor-worship". Nagas worship their ancestors and their tribal clan ancestors. The first is the religion of the Home and the second is the religion of the local divinity. Traditionally, Nagas believed that the "World of the living was everywhere ruled by the world of the dead that the individual at every moment of his existence was under ghostly supervision. All about him were invisible powers of life and death."[43] Therefore, in the old Naga life it was believed that the prosperity of the family depended upon the exact fulfillment of the duties of the ancestral cult. Therefore maintaining of the cult rested with the man not with the woman even though she shared the cult with her man.

Religious functions were performed by the village priests and chiefs. Among the Nagas the Tangkhul followed certain rituals known as *chumpha phanit* (festival). This ritual is entrusted to women to open and took out the newly harvested grain from the granaries. Before performing these rites to the goddess of wealth by women of every household eating of new rice is regarded as taboo by the Tangkhuls. Even in the paddy field women perform religious rites and prayers to the goddess of wealth (Phungkhui philava).

Among the Mao Naga tribe, there is a custom which requires a woman to remain at her husband's house for a year after his death to perform "Koyu" (departing ceremony). Again, another rite which requires a woman's participation is the feast of Merit. This feast is the most important event in ancient Mao-Naga family and the role of wife is significant during observance of gennas and other formalities. The Hasha (feast of Merit's cloth) is done by a priest to the couple in the presence of both the parents of husband and wife, Village Chief, Council of Twenty and elderly members of the husband's clan. The wife will bless all the wooden vats of wine before giving it way to the villagers.[44]

While performing feast of merit many buffaloes and bulls were killed and distributed to his sisters the legs of the animals killed. Again, the best wine will be selected from various wooden vats and several gourds of wine will be given to his sister so as to take it back to her husband's house. The said wine will be seeped and drunk by the elders of the husband's clan. That enhanced her position and strengthened her relationship with her in-laws.[45]

Maos (Sapvoma or Shifumei) worshipped only one God called Oramei or Paoravu. The Mayons also believed in the existence of a Supreme being called "Thangnang". Besides Thangnang, like any other Naga tribe, they believed in existence of Spirits called "Lae".

Among the Mao Naga tribe, to begin rice plantation, it is the duty of the women to perform a special ceremony in a particular field to propitiate the spirits of the paddy fields. The mother of the household before anyone wakes up will go to the paddy field and as soon as she reaches the paddy field, she will take a handful of paddy siblings and plant it around a small area where she will offer prayers. She would fill fresh wine in her wine-gourd and sprinkle the wine three times in the direction of the men, lion and hawk. After the ceremony the family can start planting. The Maram and Paomei Nagas also practiced similar rituals but with little variations. The religious institution of the Nagas included those customs, rites and rituals, prohibition, standard of conduct and roles primarily concerned with or justified in terms of supernatural and sacred.

Again among the Kabui Nagas, women play a major role in some special ritual ceremonies. For example, in the Banru sacrifices to God, girls and married women of the village arrange the requirements of the function helping the individual family. They also dance in the function by "putting on a special head dress known as Sanadong"[46] and by praying for the will-being of the family. Thus the Banru ceremony upholds the importance of female relatives of the Kabui society. Kabui Naga women also perform numerous religions works in their day to day life.

The Kabuis of Manipur worship Tineka Ragwang (Supreme God) and many deities. The old women mainly perform the rites, rituals and sacrifices as parts of household worship.

The Tangkhuls also believed in the existence of household deity, field deity and a Kameo for every big stones, trees, hills, rivers, etc. Since they have no place of worship such as a shrine of temple, image offerings and sacrifices were made on the roads, under the tree upon the rock, at paddy field or at other places where spirits are expected to have their abode.

In the traditional Naga society, ceremonies and rites were performed to symbolically express the importance of event occasion and belief, and also functioned to strengthen group cohesiveness. The village Chief performs village rites, the head of the clan or the old man of the clan performed rites of the community and the clan. A man could act as his own priest where there was no priest if he has learnt the art of incantation which is usually made in the time of worship or sacrifice to involve the spirits. But under no circumstances women could perform religious rites. There was also a belief that if rituals were not performed properly then that particular year natural calamities such as pests, rain, hailstorm or wind etc. would destroy the field products. Such beliefs in the supernatural being greatly determined the economic condition of not only the people but the women in particular.

"The essential rite of all worship, whether by the village through its ministrant, the Khullakpa, or by Maibas, or by private individuals in the domestic life, is a genna, a temporary disturbance of the normal course of life. Every occasion on which a sacrifice is offered is also an occasion of a genna. Yet one or two features of the system of rites and sacrifices may be mentioned here as of special interest and importance. In the first place, whether the rite is performed by the Khullakpa on behalf of the village or by the head of the household, the "celebrant" acts in a representative capacity, never alone on his own account. Then the animal offered varies, and it is notable that only domesticated animals are killed as sacrifices."[47]

Traditional norms, in fact, restricted the mobility of the people especially the women. Women were the ones to assume the rituals for agricultural practices apart from the Mawo, their roles were indeed important. But in the opinion of Ms. Aram Pamei, "there is no role such as women's role. Both should work hand in hand with love and understanding."[48]

Except in one or two sacrifices women take major part in performing the religious ceremonies. In all the family rites and rituals to propitiate the household deity, the ancestral spirits and the village deity or the supreme deity mothers perform almost all the rituals. Village priestesses also perform almost equal responsibility as the male priests. It is the mothers and grandmothers who instill the significant details of religious rites and rituals. It is through the religious power of women that social fabric of the Naga society is kept knitted for it is the women who impart intrinsic religious values such as love and compassion, truthfulness and honesty.

But in the present society, such rituals are no longer performed by majority of the people except by those who still follow the traditional religion. However, roles of both men and women remain the same. "In order to ensure good harvest women had to be careful not only in performing ritual but also the way in which they have to go about performing it. It is believed that while going to perform ritual it is a bad omen for them to meet people because if they are to talk with some bad mouthed person, that particular year animals or insects would eat up or destroy the field products and thereby cause famine."[49] Therefore, it can be seen that for the prosperity and for misfortune women were responsible to a great extent.

(V) WOMEN'S ROLE IN THE CHURCH

The coming of Christianity among the Nagas in the middle of the 19th Century brought changes in the sphere of culture and education. The role of the church in relation to women's welfare and status of women in general has been encouraging. In every church in the village or town we find women's department, known as the women's society. These women societies are very active in all churches. They are the backbone of the Church. In the Church women are appointed as deaconesses and Trustee members. The women organisation with the approval of the Church have their own programmes for worship, evangelism and philanthropic works. The members pay annual fee, membership fee etc and also contribute one or two days labour for their fund. In some local churches, every family mother contributes a handful of rice known as "Pangmashum Sam" (in Tangkhul) every week for their society. Women societies of certain churches send evangelists to unreached areas and pastors to the newly established churches. Some of the societies have self reliant projects in the form of farm, cattle rearing etc. Most of the tribals' Christianity, when one examine, is influenced by traditional culture.

Naga society being based on patriarchal system, "a sociological ethos evolved in their history from time immemorial. This age old ethos has persisted in their society, consciously or unconsciously considering women as subordinate to men with this archaic ethos they were converted into archaic Christianity."[50]

Inspite of many local Churches having women's societies many churches do not include women in the Church Assembly of the business session. But some churches allow women to take part in the discussion of the Church Assembly. However, most of the women remain silent listeners without contributing their opinions to the discussion.

Pastors and Deacon are chosen by the congregation. The pastors vocation involves administering the ordinances, educating the Church to missionary outreach, being a spiritual watchman over one's congregation and officiating at the religious ceremonies. There has not been a woman pastor in all the Naga Churches in Manipur. The only exception is found in the Church history of Bungpa Khunou Baptist Church and Nambisha Baptist Church. Church history recorded that Miss Shinningla served as the pastor of Bungpa Khunou Baptist Church from 1942 to 1949 and Miss Sarengla served as the Pastor of Nambisha Baptist Church in 1944.[51] But it was argued that their pastorship had not the full responsibility of a Pastor in the real sense, but served only as leaders of a worship congregation.

As religion played a very important role in the Naga society in every festival and on all special occasion, religious rites are essential. But these rites are abandoned and the Nagas started to celebrate "Thanks giving day"; 'Mothers Day"; "Fathers Day" Christmas, Easter and New Year. Dr. Horam in his book rightly says "The Modern Nagas has imitated a good deal of western life-style and yet they do not feel comfortable. At the same time they feel out of place because they do not fit in the traditional Naga society."[52]

This indeed is true of the Naga society. Prof. Dr. Horam further remarked that "the Nagas have accepted Christianity as their religion discarding the old religion so far so good. But it is not certainly good when you throw away your culture in the name of religion. By becoming a Christian you need not behave like the Americans or the Britishers. You need not follow the Jewish history and culture. In my utter surprise and pain in my heart, I have come to know that, some of the Nagas religion missionaries try to implant Jewish history and western way of life to Naga society. This is not only dangerous but we become a laughing stock in the eyes of the world. By becoming a Christian, you do not have to behave like Brown Sahibs or like the Americans or the Britishers. A monkey wearing a man's suite does not become a man not even semblance".[53]

However, the new tribal converts could have easier access to the administrators and the missionaries and this could necessarily give some advantage over their tribal rivals who did not have such opportunity and this could increase their power at the expenses of their neighbours.[54]

Many of the tribal customs and traditions were banned and abandoned once they become Christians. Religious rites were forbidden and replaced by Christian faith. Despite the tremendous damages inflicted on the tribal social milieus by Christianity, one must admit that Christianity brought many benefits like schools, dispensaries, idea of cleanliness, dignity of men and above all, opened vistas to the modern world.

But even today almost all the elder Church ministers are against the ordination of woman within their Church.

The notion of women's inferiority still persisted. Unfortunately, among the Manipur Nagas no women theologically trained or untrained came forward to the Church for her or their ordination. People are still influenced by their traditional religion and culture where women are forbidden to perform any religious rites.

The church must make appropriate spheres of service available to women and should ordained them to exercise the God given ministry at least in the team situations.[55]

Naga society made remarkable progresses in uplifting the status of Naga women. Some traditional attitudes towards women have lost relevancy as they are no longer practical. Mrs. Dr. T. Ninghorla Zimik remarked that "to change the mind set of the traditional ridden Naga society is a Herculean tasks for women."[56] At this transitional stage, women themselves need to project in more positive way. They should also endeavor to bring a change from the grass-root level of the society. Time has come for women and men to work hand in hand in all affairs without having social segregation and restriction for the betterment of our society and the nation.

Though Christian faith brought about new perspective and attitude there still exist some age old attitudes in certain oppressive forms. Christian tradition and its theology are male biased and exclusive and so woman's images are distorted. Re-imaging women's status and role in the society can be one of the steps to bring changes in the Church's ministry. Equal sharing should be created in the Church when men and women can work together. There should be no distinction in the basis of gender. Women need to empower themselves to protect, assert their rights and stand for justice.

Christianity educated them to take up new roles. Their enlightenment prompted them to adapt to better life style, better health and hygiene. Therefore, the Church must immerse in a total struggle of women and to empower them to build a better and fuller human community where women can experience total liberation and full human-hood by participating together.

Naga women as seen today are wiser and more determined about the removal of the oppressive structure of the society. Many traditional practices have been discarded and some kept, but the practices like the inheritance law which causes greater evil are still upheld as positive part of culture and tradition. The fact that women are not subordinate beings but are also human beings created in the image of God along with men must be recognized.

References

1. S.S. Chib; "Caste, Tribes and Culture of India; Vol. 8; North Eastern India, 1984; p. 160.
2. Fading Histories : Journal of the Asiatic Society, 1984.
3. Statistical Handbook of Manipur, 1982.
4. Ibid.

5. E.W. Dun, Gazetteer of Manipur, Vivek Publishing House, Delhi, 1975; p. 28.
6. R.K. Das, "Manipur Tribal Scene"; p. 6.
7. R.R. Shimray: Origin and Culture of the Nagas; Samsoh Publication, New Delhi; 1985; p. 7.
8. G.Kabui : Genesis of the Ethnoses of Nagas and Kuki-Chin, Published by N.S.F. (Naga Students Federation).
9. R.K. Das, Ibid.
10. Jyotsana Chatterji, (ed.) The Women's Decade, 1975-1985, Banhi Series, J.W.P., ISPCK, Delhi; p. 14.
11. A.J. Moffatt Mills, "Angami life and Custom", The Nagas in the Nineteenth Century, Verrier Elwin(ed), Oxford University Press, London, 1969.
12. Johnstone: Op.cit.
13. T.C.Hudson: The Naga Tribes of Manipur; B.R. Publishing Corporation, Delhi : p. 6.
14. R. Horam : Naga Polity, reprinted 1992; p. 46.
15. Personal interview of Ms. Grace Satsang, President, Naga Women's Union, Manipur.
16. M. Horam, Nagas Old Ways New Trends, Cosmo Publications, New Delhi, 1988; p. 41.
17. Furer Haimendorf C. Jon : The Naked Nagas; Methuen & Company, London, 1939.
18. V. Free Paothing : Status of Tangkhul Women; p. 7.
19. Dr. Hunibou Newmai : The Status of Women in Zeliangrong society in "Women in Naga society" edited by Dr. Lucy Zehol; p. 44.
20. R.R. Shimray, Op.Cit.; p. 168.
21. R.R. Shimray, Ibid; p. 169.
22. N. Sanajaoba, Manipur Past and Present, Vol. III; p. 401.
23. R.R. Shimray, Ibid; p. 199.
24. R.R. Shimray, Op.Cit; p. 169.
25. Z.V. Free Paothing : Op. Cit.; p. 68.
26. Maiya Gachiu, Hao Miun Ngashan Kala Tangkhul Khararchan, Imphal, 1988; p. 103.

27. Ghose, G.K. : Tribes and Culture : Manipur and Nagaland, Vol.3; Ashish Publishing House, New Delhi, Chapter 8, Zewi Naga; p. 51.
28. Personal interview : Mrs. Khanangla Keishing, 84 years (Retired School Teacher) Bungpa Village, Ukhrul District.
29. Raisunriang (Newslink): Naga Women's Union, Manipur; II Issue, March, 1996.
30. Z.V. Paothing, Op. Cit., p. 70.
31. Personal interview : Valley Rose, Editor, "Aya Daily" in Tangkhul on 10th October, 2007.
32. Raisunriang (Newslink): Naga Women's Union, Manipur; III Issue, Oct,1997; p. 10.
33. Luithui, L. and Nandita Haskar, Nagaland file, Lancer international, New Delhi, 1984; p. 230.
34. K. Terhuia : "Status of Women in Naga Society", "Nagas" 90 (Guwahati Literature Committee, 1990); p. 19.
35. Clark, M.M., A corner in India, American Baptist Publication Society, Philadelphia, 1907; p. 23.
36. U.G. Bower: Naga Path; London, 1950; p. 23.
37. Personal interview of Mr. K. Prongo Keishing, Retired Government Officer.
38. Personal interview of Ms. Grace Satsang, President, Naga Women's Union, Manipur.
39. M. Horam : Op. Cit; p. 70.
40. Varrier Edwin : Nagaland, 1961; p. 15.
41. Dr. Vinita Kaul, Women and the Wind of Change, Gyan Publishing House, 2000; p. 163.
42. S. Sarkar : Psycho-Dynamics of Tribal Behaviour, Bookland Private Limited, Calcutta, 1965: p. 6.
43. M. Horam : Op. Cit.; p. 13.
44. N. Sanajaoba, Manipur Past and Present, Vol.III; p. 425 (The Mao Naga – K.S. Benjamin Banee).
45. N. Sanajaoba : Op. Cit.; Vol. III; p. 427.
46. Gangmumei Kamei: "A History of Zeliangrong Nagas"; Spectrum Publication, Guwahati, Delhi, 2004; p. 309.

47. T.C. Hudson : The Naga Tribes of Manipur, B.R. Publishing Corporation, Delhi; p. 139.
48. Personal interview with Ms. Aram Pamei on 23.11.2007.
49. Dr. Adino Vitso, Customary Law and Women, The Chakhesang Naga Regency Publications, New Delhi; p. 71.
50. Z.V. Free Paothing : Status of Tangkhul Women; p. 84.
51. Ringshi K. : E, History of ETNBA, Imphal, 1980; pp. 56, 57.
52. Dr. M. Horam, Op. Cit.; 1988; p. 82.
53. Dr. M. Horam, The Changing Culture and The Naga Society; pp. 26-27.
54. Ibid.
55. John Scott, Issue Facing Christian Today, Gospel Literature Service, Bombay, 1981; p. 254.
56. Dr. T. Ninghorla Zimik, Seminar Paper on "Social Status and the Role of Naga Women in the Traditional Naga Society."

6

Women and Health

Women's health plays an important role in determining the health of the future population because women's health has an intergenerational effect.

The culture, traditions and custom which have its roots in patriarchal system and male biased philosophy have been suppressing the welfare and development of women since pre-civilization period. Women in general are not expressive but rather silent in their own cases of health related issues.

To be healthy requires good food, mental and physical rest, economic back-up and sound knowledge of health. The deterioration of health care system and the rapid spread of diseases include those associated with malnutrition and inadequate water supply systems. "In India 100,000 mothers die every year and this constitute 20 per cent of all maternal deaths in the world".[1]

India has never had a clear cut policy for women's health. But a range of policy decisions has directly or indirectly influenced women's health.

Women's health covers morality, morbidity, nutritional status and reproductive health. Linked to these are environmental degradation, violence and occupational hazards, all of which have implications for women's health.

While the cutbacks in the social sectors were an important part of the structural adjustment programme, a recent work has demonstrated that if health care has to be improved, public health expenditure must be increased. The report of the committee on the "Status of women in India" in 1974 "towards equality" focused among other things on the declining sex ratio in India attracted international attention.

The sixth five year plan (1980-85) attempted to integrate and interlink issues related to women across sectors to guide the various ministries dealing with women's issues.

The report of the National Commission on Self-Employed Women and Women in Formal Sectors (1988) recognized the occupational health hazards of women.

The Government of India undertook programmes for Women's health like Maternity and Child Health (MCH), Family Planning Programme (FPP) and Nutrition and Immunization programmes. These were brought into the frame of the family and transformed into a reproductive and child health (RCH) strategy. Another programme is the Integrated Child Development Scheme (ICDS) which was started in the year 1975. Unfortunately, in Manipur the policy of declaration on health by the WHO (World Health Organization) and emphasis given by the Government of India for improvement of health still remains a distant dream for poorer section of the society. Most of the Health centres in Manipur, District Hospitals and Health Sub-centres are far below the required standard.

Moreover, the present political scenario and conflict situations make Doctors and Health Workers to excuse themselves of not going to rural remote areas or places. Apart from this problem, in Manipur private run Health institutions are becoming more popular day by day whereas Government run Hospitals and centres are decreasing its standard even at the heart of the capital city Imphal. There are two state level hospitals which has more than 200 beds each. There are Primary Health Centres (PHSC), Hospitals run by Non-Governmental organizations and churches in Imphal and Churachandpur. There are Nature Cure Hospitals also in Manipur.

In the valley the existing health care institutions are functioning but in the hills due to shortage of funds and due to prolonged armed conflict most of them are defunct now. The World Health Report, 2004 noted that with the exception of Shri Lanka all the countries in South Asia fall in the 'high child and high adult' mortality stratum. Women's access to Health and Health seeking behaviour is affected by their low economic status, social norms and cultural values.[2]

In Manipur the incidence of Reproductive tract infections (RTIs) and Sexually Transmitted Diseases (STDs) remain high and the spread of H.I.V. (Human Immune Virus) infection is increasing at alarming rate. Communicable diseases such as Tuberculosis, Malaria, and Dysentery are also major health problems especially in rural areas. During illness fewer women than men seek and received treatment. There is a gender asymmetry in the utilization of health services. Early and forced marriages, young motherhood continue and malnutrition, anemia and higher morbidity persists. As a result young adolescent girls who discontinue their education and vocational training are denied information about their bodies, thereby constituting a life cycle of deprivation and discrimination resulting in a continuum of health related vulnerabilities for women and young girls.

Poverty, food insecurity and lack of information further weaker women's health status. Complications following abortions are a major cause of maternal mortality.[3]

The Indian National Health Policy, 2001 gives high priority to Women's health. The Reproductive and Child Health (RCH) programme (Second phase started in 2003) is designed to meet women's need across their life span. The National Population Policy, 2000, National Health Policy, 2001 and the Tenth Five Year Plan (2002-2007) placed a special emphasis on adolescent's needs and empowerment of women. It has been emphasized that the infant mortality rate and maternal mortality ratio are unacceptably high and need special attention.

Violence against women is beginning to be addressed as a public health concern. An initiative in India, the family violence prevention fund seek to ensure that women who come to a partner hospital in Mumbai. They are asked about their possible experience of sexual abuse or violence and are offered councelling and care in case of need. In the context of ante-Natal services local health practices including access to traditional systems of medicine and practitioners, home based remedies, birth attendants and often demonized shamans or witch doctors are accessed in many parts of South Asia.

These are all issues which need to be factored into reforms of public health system in the region to strengthen preventive programmes.[4]

Therefore, it is women who have been the primary health care provider at home and possessed knowledge of home remedies and folk medicines. Ordinary village women know how to manage many common health problems using local resources and home remedies.

However, women's healing knowledge has been largely overlooked by the 'Development' process. They are not recognized as healers and the indigenous healing systems practiced are today on the verge of extinction.

Aggressive commercialization and pharmaceuticalization of health care has only made access to health care by the poor more difficult.

Violence and sexual coercion have a severe impact in increasing women's vulnerability to HIV/AIDS. "Women are often burdened in the care economy exclusively as care givers rather than as receiver of care".[5]

Manipur is one of six states identified by the Government of India as high HIV Prevalence state. The HIV prevalence rate among the women who attended ante-natal clinics in the state is 13 out of 1000 (according to 2005 sentinel surveillance report of MACS). It is very dangerous that HIV/AIDS is steadily attacking the innocent women of the state who do not indulge in risky behaviours like drug injection and sex selling works.[6]

Out of the total 161,813 blood samples tested for HIV upto August, 2006 there are 23,856 cases of HIV infection, 5323 of them are women. Majority of them are housewives who get the virus from their husbands.

In a Manipuri Film, "Ningol Pukning", based on AIDS awareness depicts the social evil stigma and discrimination which is fuelling the AIDS epidemic in most underdeveloped and developing countries of the world.

When a woman is found positive on HIV, there is an escalation of domestic violence by family members especially after the death of the spouse/partner. Many of them are thrown out of their marital homes and deprived of their property rights and maintenance and have to constantly struggle and fight for what is their very own.

Women face a great deal of occupational health hazards in the work that they do, be it informal sector or formal sector.

"Due to excessive use of pesticides in agriculture workers are often found suffer from visual impairment, dislike of bright lights, night blindness, mental disturbances, anxiety insomnia and depression.[7]

Again women living in forest areas due to deforestation lost their source of nutrition, medicinal herbs, plants, roots and fruits which led to increase in diseases and mortality in women.

Environment degradation has serious consequences on women's health. Due to deforestation rural women are also losing valuable working hours. Each day looking for fuel and fodder take its toll on the health of women which causes body ache, joint pains and other physical problems. Over a period of time due to carrying of heavy load on the head postural defects of the neck, spine and pelvis may develop. Again, women suffer due to the increase in population which deprived them of privacy and complicate health problems in the absence of toilet facilities.

In around conflict situation women's health suffer too because they are targeted both by state and non state actors. It has given rise to many women-headed household. Often many of the widows resort to drinking liquor, drugs or even go to prostitution to earn money for their livelihood. This also greatly increases their risks of getting infected with HIV/AIDS, sexual slavery and the spread of sexually transmitted diseases.

Taxes taken by armed groups cause price-hike of medicine and many poor common people especially women are not able to afford essential drugs. Due to prolonged armed conflict large number of women are not able to have any access to health care even pre-natal and post-natal care.

Lastly, the main concerns of women in Manipur are increasing rape, unwanted pregnancies and lack of decision making power of women. Another concern is the rising addiction to alcohol and high prevalence of HIV/AIDS in which women are vulnerable.

In the hill areas women are sandwiched between the police/armed forces who seek information about insurgents and the sick and wounded insurgents who seek the villagers help. Many women are tortured and sexually abused by the armed personnel. Again, excessive gun fighting among factional groups has caused much trauma for the general public and especially among the women.

Therefore, it is time to remove ignorance from their minds of the public in order to get rid of stigma and discrimination. Only education and awareness about good health will be able to bring happiness to our society.

Non Governmental Organisations have an important role to play in promotion of the health of women. This must be undertaken not only by women's organisation but by those which have mixed membership and are working in the wider range of social development.[8]

According to Neeti Malhotra, gender sensitive intervention appreciated the differences between the needs of men and women and finds ways to meet those needs differently. A step up are gender transformative interventions which not only recognise the distinction between the needs of men and women but also create conditions by which women and men can examine the damaging aspects of gender norms and experiment with new behaviours to create more equitable roles and relationships. In the end of the continuum are structural interventions, which go beyond health interventions to reduce gender inequalities through empowering women and girls by increasing their access to economic and social resources.[9] Therefore, women's health is inextricably linked to women's rights and their status in a community.

Some suggestions for the improvement of the health of women are given below :

1. Women's access to health care and information and related services must be within affordable.

2. Preventive measures should be promoted for women's health.

3. Traditional system of medicine should be promoted.

4. Research and disseminate information on women's health must be promoted.

5. There must be co-operation between Govt. and Non-Governmental Organisations and the community.

6. More self Help Groups should be raised in order to bring awareness of HIV/AIDS among women and help to empower them negotiate condom use.

7. Male responsibilities must be emphasized.

8. Gender sensitization for elimination against women in all spheres.

9. Increase in resourcês and monitor follow up for women health should be made.

10. Women's participation in peace process needs to be strengthened etc.

11. Women should be empowered because empowerment of women is due to the key factor for meeting specific health need of women.

References

1. WHO Bulletin in 2002.

2. Positive Speaking UNIFEM et al, 2003. (United Nations Development Fund for Women).
3. Abortion Assessment Project – India Summary and Key Findings CEHAT, 2004 in Progress of South Asian Women, 2005; p. 20.
4. Gender Dimentions of HIV/AIDS UNIFEM, UN AIDS, 2004.
5. Lawyers collective HIV/AIDS unit, 2001; Positive speaking, CFAR/ PWN + UNIFEM, 2003 in progress of South Asian Women, 2005; p. 23.
6. The Sangai Express, Tuesday, 24th Oct., 2006.
7. Fourth World Conference of Women, Beijing, 1995, Country Report; p. 88.
8. Contributed by Avabai B. Wadai, President Family Planning Association of India.
9. Women's Work Health and Empowerment; Edited by Anjali Gandhi; Published by Aakar Books, Delhi 2006; p. 188.

7

Conclusion

In the preceding chapters, the roles of women of different communities in politics, economy, religion and society have been discussed. The roles played by women changed from time to time according to the given situations and circumstances. Women in every society play certain roles. The position of women in a society can be identified by examining the roles and activities performed by them in different fields.

Meitei women have a distinctively higher position and status with greater responsibilities than women of other societies. Her role in the society is very unique. Her role as an economic contribution and the high ritual status of priestesses in the core of the religious system are two unique features in the male oriented society. The traditional roles of Meitei women are too deep rooted to be subverted by the Brahmanic influence. Unlike in other parts of India, there is no restriction for women to participate in religious Kirtans or festivals observed in the temples. Hindu values failed to diminish the strength of women's public role.

The most unusual feature in the institution of the Maibis is that these women who are ordained as priests of the Meitei core religion do not form a sub-culture, rather they are an integral part of the Meitei culture. They are accepted in the existing social order of the Meitei society. Manjusri Chaki Sircar rightly remarks that "A women in Meitei society is indeed a recognized citizen of the community by virtue of her own identity as a member of the Khulang (the rice cultivation team) the Marup (the credit association), the Nupi Pala (religious association for women) and various other activities, regardless of her marital status". Women provide supplementary income but she can also use her capital for economic autonomy in times of need. It is found that women's control over production and resources extended beyond the home.

Among the Meitei Pangal women, the influence of Meitei culture is so great that they speak meitei-lon (Meitei language) and even wear Meitei Phaneks. The only difference is that they fasten their phanek under their right breasts while the Meiteis fasten their phanek under the left breast.

Every Pangal woman generally covers her head with a piece of cloth (Khudei). Purdah system which seems to be very strange in Manipur is now gaining, new ground recently where few women use a new form of Burkha which covers the body and face. Unlike in other states of India, Meitei Pangal women generally go out without veils in crowded market and in the fields. Pardah system depended on the nature of the family and locality. Education is still not given to all women except theological lessons. Therefore, from our empirical data we find that the status of Pangal women is still very low in Manipur. Poverty and the daily needs of the family compel her to come out of the home.

Inspite of the rising rate of literacy in Manipur, Meitei Pangal women are still way behind in the field of education.

But in the present day, Manipuri Meitei Pangal women formed many organisations at the local level as well as the state level for the development of their society.

Inspite of their lack of education we find many Meitei Pangal women in Zilla Parishads as Councillors, Pradhans and Members in different tier of Local Self Government.

Meitei Pangal society is now gradually changing for the better even though religion, politics, society and economic forces do not support their development. Therefore, voluntary action is the most important measure to improve the contemporary ethos. Efforts should begin with awareness generation and social education. Women should be given freedom from the chain of social bindings and traditions. The persistence of a particularly entrenched form of patriarchy in which only man have rights, equality and unlimited accers to public space has meant that apart from a very small urban female educated, the vast majority of Meitei Muslim women have experienced illiteracy, poor health and subordination.

Among the tribes, the roles of women are almost the same. Their main occupation is agriculture. The Kukis formed groups called 'LOM' which is one of the most important organisation concerned with the economic relations among the Kukis. This collective labour force gave the Kuki women a sense of responsibilities and peaceful co-existence among themselves. It contributed greatly to the socio-economic development of the village in particular and the society in general. Things have changed with the coming of the British and the Kukis have realized, with the coming of western education, the importance of education and having material possession. The labour inputs and time spent by both men and women is comparatively the same with regard to agricultural activities. Educated women working in different fields contribute much to the family's income, but they have no right of inheritance.

In the Kuki society, maternal bond is not broken as many cultural rites and ceremonies are observed even after a woman got married and left her maternal home. Again, the custom of paying Longman (Payment towards her corpse) to the nearest male relative shows an important position and prominent place held by her in the society.

In the Kuki society widows and divorced women suffer no social disabilities. Some customs prevent women to exercise power in the family matters in decision making but in practice the husband consult his wife in all matters before taking any decision. Traditionally women were not allowed in the village council.

A striking thing we discovered from our empirical research is that there are some women who hold chieftainship or chairmanship after the death of their husbands among the Kukis.

Kuki women took part with men in most of the religious festivals and ceremonies e.g. Chang-ai. This feast is conducted under her sole supervision and direction. Inspite of many cultural and traditional restrictions imposed on women, Kuki women are becoming more liberal and are faring as well as their male counterparts in their academic and professional pursuits.

Christianity certainly has brought modernization and irreversible changes for the Kukis.

Kuki women's role in the church is an active one. However, their participation in leadership role as well as decision making body seems to be very minimal. Their roles seem to be confined only in secondary roles of assistance. When the Kuki Baptist Convention, for the first time, ordained a woman in 1998 that was also done with the condition that she should not get married. Many Churches today allow women to be represented within the decision making bodies of the Church, yet, the attitude of most men towards women is far from the ideal. Thankfully, the Church on its part is slowly promoting the welfare and status of women which were not given much importance because if the strong age-old traditional concept man being superior to woman. Kuki society in general is more willing to accept the multiple roles of women.

The Naga women on the other hand experienced improvement in their status and playing new roles within the purview of male dominated church and a patriarchal society. The Naga culture(s) has been resilient but it has learned to adapt to the changing context and to accept the many changes in the society in homes and in churches. Education and Christianity has provided them with incentive for upward mobility. But sad to say that it is the same Christianity/ Church that is still reluctant to admit women to equal status and partnership with men in ordained ministry.

Christianity has improved the life of the tribals in general and in particular the life of women, yet it is ironic that the place where the gospel is supposed to be the based on life has become the place where discrimination is largely seen. Women as seen today in Manipur are wiser and more determined about the removal of the oppressive structure. But there is a great need for motivation to actually get involved and to empower them so that they can experience total liberation and full womanhood by participating together.

In Manipur, women from different communities still retain their own cultures and traditions. This helps to fill the gap between the modern and the ancient.

It is high time for the patriarchal society to realize that women's emancipation is directed not against men but aimed at the untapped resources of the society to make the society richer.

Empowerment of women enhances their ability to influence the direction of social change to create a better social and economic order. Increasing the participation of women in stimulating economic activity and producing jobs gives them the requisite influence in the larger political and policy decision making framework. Women are more and more aware of the community's need. Concern and interests are different from that of men.

Therefore, equal opportunity must be given at work at the grass-root level. Women should be viewed as a dynamic promoter of social transformation rather than as passive recipients of help. In fact, empirical evidences indicate that education, employment and ownership rights of women tend to have a significant influence on their ability to control their environment and contribute to economic development. Women's intellectual capacities are not inferior to those of men have been proven from time to time by women themselves.

Being a conflict ridden and trouble torn state, creativity is restricted and as living conditions worsened for the people especially women, empowering women and making them aware of their rights seems a distant dream. But great leadership emanates from the ability to dream. Nothing is impossible if we believe in our abilities and work to realize our dream, we will achieve our rightful place in the world.

It is true that throughout history, patriarchy has oppressed women and excluded them from the centres of power. Women were excluded from participating in cultural dialogue that shapes reality. Manipuri women refused to fix themselves strictly inside the roles "Pigeon holed" for them. The discourses used by women in Manipuri may seem in adequate but these discourses have allowed them to express reality in their best capacity. Despite its patriarchal bent, Manipuri women chose to be productive not only within their domestic homes but also in the outside male-dominated public world. Women in Manipur are still continued to be the custodians of their society.

Given the vital role that a woman plays in our society in the absence of adequate levels of female literacy, economic opportunities, the risks increases for the society as a whole, that the next generation of children would be ill-prepared.

There is much a woman can do in a male dominated society. Being a woman is a handicap sometimes but the woman herself must work hard to protect the rights of her peers. The future look brought for young Manipuri women who are ready to step out of their societal "Cocooning".

Therefore, great emphasis should be laid on raising the status of women, enhancing awareness of the problems of women, creating mass consciousness about women rights, implementing national programme of training and employment of women and also enabling women to participate with equality in socio-economic development and nation building etc. Educating women at par with men will surely bring harmony in the society we live in.

Women's contribution in society, economic, politics and religious aspects should be recognised and they must be supported by the family and encouraged to march forward for a better society. Men may be the head of the family but the women folk form the backbone of the society. On the whole, men and women should realize that they are not opposing forces in society but complimentary members for the harmony of the society.

In our society today, inspite of the spread of education and knowledge a dichotomy still exists in women's position inside and outside the home. They may be submissive and docile at home but vocal, mobile and a powerful force outside of it, ready to fight for just causes in the society.

Bibliography

(A) Primary Sources

1. Administration Report of Manipur Agency, 1874-79.
2. Census of India, 1931; Part-I, Vol. XI.
3. Government of India's letter No. 43261A, dt. 1st Oct, 1919.
4. Government of Manipur (Directorate for Development of Tribals and Backward Classes, Manipur), Draft Eighth Five Year Plan, 1990-95 and 1991-92 and Recast Annual Plan, 1990-91, Imphal, August, 1990.
5. Government of Manipur (Directorate of Information and Public Relations), Manipur Today, Imphal 1992-2001.
6. Government of Manipur (Directorate of Rural Development and Panchayati Raj), Panchayati Raj, Vol. 295 & 298, Imphal, Nov.,1994 and Feb., 1995.
7. Janab Khan, Ipham, M.A. (ed.) "Nongsamei" (Puya), Imphal, 1973.
8. L. Ibohal and N. Khelchandra (ed.): Cheitharol Kumbaba, Manipuri Sahitya Parishad, Imphal, 1989.
9. Manipur Administration Report, 1913-14.
10. Manipur Administration Report, 1919-20.

11. O. Bhogeshwor (ed), Ningthourol Lambuba, Vol.1, Imphal 1967.

12. Personal communication : November 9, 1977.

13. Political Agent Diary, 10th February, 1986 (State Archives).

14. Report of Webster, For & Poll Department, 1919.

15. Report of Webster, Secretary to the Chief Commissioner of Assam to the Secretary, Government of India.

16. Secretary to the Governor of Assam's letter No. 93 dated 22nd April, 1919 to the Government of India.

17. Seminar Papers and unpublished manuscripts.

18. Social-Economic Survey of Meitei Pangal – Directorate of Economics and Statistics, Manipur, 2004.

19. Statistical Handbook of Manipur, 1982.

20. Unrecorded conventional Customary Law practices and oral history.

(a) Newspapers

1. Assam Tribune (English), Guwahati.

2. Freedom (English), Imphal.

3. Hindustan Times (English), Delhi.

4. Huiyen Lanpao (Manipuri), Imphal.

5. Imphal Free Press (English), Imphal.

6. Naharolgi Thoudang (Manipuri), Imphal.

7. Poknapham (Manipuri), Imphal.

8. Sangai Express (English), Imphal.

9. The Telegraph (English), Imphal.

10. Thoudang (Manipuri), Imphal.

11. Times of India (English), Delhi.

(b) Journals and Periodicals, Published Materials, etc.

1. 69th Anniversary of the Kuki Rebellion, 1917-19, 1985.

2. Accountability to the World's Women Progress of South Asian Women, 2005.

3. A. J. Shah : Glimpses of World Religion, Jaico, Bombay, 1990.

4. Bethy R. Schort : "The Sociological Study of Religion".

5. Ch. Shilaramani : "Manipurda Lairik Haibi Nupishingi Thoudang", Chingkhei Hunba, Vol. 32, M. Rajen, Oct. 1995.

6. D.R. Dutt, An outline of World Civilization, New Delhi, 1968.

7. Dr. N. Tomba : Nature and Culture : "The Sanamahi and Leimarel", Orient Vision, Vol.1, Issue 1, National Research Centre, Manipur, Imphal, Dec., 1994.

8. Eastern Panorama, News Magazine of North East, Vol. IV, No.12, November, 2006.

9. Fading Histories, Journal of the Asiatic Society, 1984.

10. Fourth World Conference on Women, Beijing, 1995 (Country Report).

11. G. Kabui, Genesis of the Ethnoses of the Nagas and Kuki Chin, Naga Students' Federation.

12. Gamgrade K.D.: "Gandhi and Empowerment of Women", Gandhi Marg, Vol. 22, No. 4; Anupam Mishra, Delhi, Jan-March, 2001.

13. Health Rights, Women lives, Challenges and Strategies for Movement Building : 10th International Women and Health Meeting, 2005.

14. Indian Women's Health Concerns : 10th International Women and Health Meeting, 2005.

15. International Women's Right Action Watch, The Women's Watch, Vol.13, No.2; Humphrey Institute, University of Minnesota, U.S.A., January, 2000.

16. J. Shakespear: The Religion of Manipur Folklore, Transformation of the Folklore Society, Vol. XXIV; No.IV, Dec, 1913.

17. Jyotsana Chatterji (ed): The Women's Decade Banhi Series, J.W.P., ISPCK.

18. K. Terhuia, Status of Women in Naga Society, "Nagas", Guwahati Literature Committee, 1990.

19. Ksh. Bimola: "Nupilan Amasung Houjikki Manipuri Nupee", Eikhoigi Panthung, Vol. 2, United People Front, Imphal, Dec. 2001.

20. Ksh. Bimola: Manipurgi Nupeeshingda Modernization Purakliba", Sanathong, Vol. 2, No. 4, Imphal, June, 1995.

21. Kut Souvenirs, 2004-2007.

22. M.C. Arun, Female Writers Alienation and Manipuri Society, "Echo", MUSU, Nov, 1992.

23. M.F. Quadir, Muslims of North East India, Souvenir North East India, 15th Century Hijri Era Celebration, 7 & 8th, 1981.

24. M.H. Khan and Pankaj Nithori : Indigenous People and Co-operative Development in the North East India, First edition, 2000.

25. N. Joykumar : "Khunnaida Nupigi Thoudang", Sanathong, Vol. 2, No.10; Priyadarshini Book House Publication, Imphal, 1995.

26. Naga People's Movement for Human Rights, Vol. III, No. 6, Quarterly Publication Dec, 2007.

27. Narayana Usha "Condition of Women Over the Last Fifty Years", Mainstream, Vol. 35, No.16 : Sumit Chakravorty, New Delhi, April, 1998.

28. O. Tomba : The need to rewrite Manipuri History, Imphal, 1993.

29. Progress of South Asian Women, 2005: United Nations Development Fund for Women.

30. Quoted in Souvenir – Golden Jubilee Celebration of Azad Hind Government, 21st Oct., 1993.

31. Raisuriang (News-link), 1996-2001. Naga Women's Union, Manipur.

32. Ringshi K.: History of ETNBA, 1980.

33. Ruth B. Edwards : "The Case for Women Ministry"; London, 1989.

34. S.Q.R. Ilyas, Sun News Bulletin, Vol.V, No. 5 & 6, Aligarh, 1982.

35. Saheli, News Letter, 8th March, 1997.

36. Salam Irene, "Manipur Muslim Women" (Research Study), Manipur University.

37. T. Ito : "Meitei Nupida Nupashingee Mityeng"; Ahongba, Vol. I, No. 2, Imphal, June, 1995.

38. The Nagas, Monthly, Journal October, 1980.

39. Tyson Lois : Critical Theory Today, Second Edition, 2006.

40. United Nations, Women at a Glance, Department of Public Relations, New York, May, 1997.

41. United Nations: The United Nations and the Status of Women, Department of Public Relation, New York, May, 1995.

42. Wahida Nainar, "Muslim Women's Views on Person Laws" (The Influence of Socio-Economic Factors), December, 2000.

43. William A. Lessa and Evon Z. Vogt : Reader in Comperative Religion, 4th Edition.

44. Women in Armed Conflict Situations (A Study of North East Network), Guwahati, 2005.

45. Women Studies in India (Some Perspectives), edited by Maithreyi Krishna Raj.

46. Women Watch, Vol. 3, Issue 1, National Federation on Indian Women.

47. Women's Work Health and Empowerment, edited by Anjali Gandhi, 2006.

48. Yojna, Vol. 49, May, 2006.

49. Young Muslim Digest (Monthly), Bangalore.

(c) Non-English

1. Arim Lungleng Raikhan, Talla Kasarnao, Saklong Pheikashok Pheikashoknei Bible, 1991.

2. Gachiu Maya, Hao Miun Ngashan Kala Tangkhul Khararchan, Imphal, 1988.

3. Haokip, Letkhojam : "Thempu Ho THU (A magicl verses/ chants of the traditional priest) 1st ed, May, 2000.

4. Lunkim Dr. T. Kuki Inpi (Kuki Government) published by the Author.

5. Misao, Jangkhosat, C : Kukite Chondan (Custom and Culture of the Kukis), Sadar Hills, Kangpokpi, Manipur.

6. Sagolsem Taruni Devi, Manipuri Thouna Phabi Nupising, 2002.

7. Sitlhou, Jamkithang, Thadou Puchon Pachon (Thadou Culture and Custom).

8. Songate L. Hranglian : Hmar Chanchin (Hmar History), Churachandpur, 1977.

(B) Seminar Papers and Unpublished Sources

1. Akhum Khare : Tangkhul Thochan.

2. Binarani Th : "The Role of Women Organisation as pressure Group in Imphal".

3. Ch. Jamini : Status of Women in Manipuri (Meitei) society: - Seminar on Gender Equity, organized by Adult Continuing Education and Extension, M.U., 2000.

4. Changsan N.M.: "The Prophetic Role of Women in O.T. and its significance for the Kuki Women in the New Millennium", B.D. Thesis, ETC Jorhat, 1997.

5. David Younggi Cho : "Don't be afraid to empower Women" – Sermon preached at Lawn of Beauty Conference Italy, 1999.

6. Dr. Kunjani Devi : "Muslim Women's Status in the family and society in Manipur".

7. Dr. Md. Kheiruddin Shah,: The Status of Muslim Women in Manipur State : Organised by Child Welfare Ashram, Jiribam, 4-6 Jun, 2007.

8. Dr. T. Ninghorla Zimik : "Social Status and the Role of Naga Women in the Traditional Naga Society.

9. Gangte Tingneichong : Status of Women in Kuki Society; Department of History, M.U. 2007.

10. Gangte, M. Priyadarshni : Status of Women in Mizo Society – A two day seminar on the Social Status of

Women of North East India, sponsored by Gandhi Smiriti and Darshan Samiti, New Delhi, M.U.

11. Goswami M.C. & C.B. Singh : Patron and Patroness client, Relation in Thanga Marketing Organisation; Bulletin of the Anthropology Department, Gauhati University, 1972.

12. Henkhovum Haolai: "A historical study of the develop of Christianity among the Kukis of North Cachar Hills District of Assam with special reference to K.C.C. Church, Synod and its musicological implications.

13. Irene Salam : Women in Manipur – Problems and Prospects of Retrieval, North East Regional Seminar on "Feminist Scholarship in North East India, Retrieving and Reconstructing the Women, NEHU, 2007.

14. K. Gailangam : Socio-Cultural Restriction on Women in the Tribal Society of Manipur, Gender Equity, Organized by Adult Continuing Education and Extension, M.U. 28-30 March, 2000.

15. Kipgen Tinkholhing : The Leadership Role of the Women in Fourth Gospel in the eyes of the Kuki Women in Manipur", 2004.

16. Kipgen Tinkholhing : The Status and Role of Kuki Women in the Church and society (B.D. Thesis, ETC Jorhat, 1997.

17. Kipgen, Sheikhohao : Political and Economic History of the Kukis of Manipur : Ph.D. Thesis submitted to M.U., Department of History, 2005.

18. Ksh. Bimola : Manipuri Women in the Beginning of the 21st Century – Seminar on Women in the North-East Challenges and Opportunities in the 21st Century, organized by Women's Studies Research Centre, Guwahati University, Guwahati, 2-4 March, 2002.

19. Ksh. Bimola "Manipur Women in the present Day Society, "An observation, Women Vol. II, MUWWA, Imphal, 1996.

20. Laldinpui Audrey : Women and Decision Making – A study of two villages in Mizoram".- Paper for Regional Seminar on Feminist Scholarship in North East India, NEHU, 2007.

21. Lalriemsiem : Position of Women in Mizo Society – A Historical Study, M.Phil Thesis, M.U.

22. M. Rita : Meira Paibi Movement in Manipur XXII NEIHA, Annual Conference, Tezpur, Nov., 2001.

23. M.C. Arun: Social Status on Women of North East India, 3-4 June, 2005. at Senate Hall, M.U., Imphal.

24. Mairembam Rita : A Socio Political Study of Women in Manipur : Ph.D. Thesis submitted to M.U., Department of Political Science, 2002.

25. Mani Babu, M. : "Meetei Women's Working Team in Agriculture : A Non-nuclear approach on an organisation in production ; Anthropology Department, Dibrugarh University.

26. Md. Ahmad Ali Shah : "A Brief Historical Study of Religion and Society of the Pangals of Manipur." Dissertation submitted to M.U. for award of the Degree of Master of Philosophy.

27. Md. Riyas Ahmed Shah : "Status of Muslim Women in Manipur".

28. Mrs. Laljan Begum: "Muslim Women's Educational Status in Manipur"- Seminar paper presented in State Level Seminar .

29. N. Joykumar : Women and Their Participation in the Social and Economic Life of Manipur; - Seminar on Women's Movement in Manipur – 20th Century-

Organized by Department of History, M.U., Imphal, 26-27 March, 2002.

30. Neihsial Tualchin : History of the Zomis – Ph.D. Thesis submitted to M.U., Department of History, 1993.

31. Rev. Prim Vaiphei : "Church Growth Among Hill Tribes in Manipur – North East India.", Imphal, 1986.

32. Sina Khayi : "Cultural Significance of Tribal Costumes in Modern Times" : MUTSU, March, 1996.

33. Singson D: The Kuki Christian Church of India (Thesis submitted for Degree of Missiology), 1985.

34. Social Status of Women, 3-4 June, 2005 at Senate Hall of North East India, M.U. Imphal.

35. T.S. Gangte : Seminar Paper, MUTSU, 2001.

36. Y. Amar : Women in Manipur, A Real Backbone of the Economy, Seminar on Gender Equity, organized by Adult Continuing Education and Extension, M.U. 28-30 March, 2000.

(d) Persons Interviewed

1. Dr. Ninghorla Zimik, Lecturer, G.P. Women's College, Imphal.
2. Dr. (Mrs.) Priyadarshni M. Gangte, Old Lambulane.
3. Dr. Ch. Jamini Devi, Chairman, Manipur State Commission for Women.
4. Dr. R.K. Tamphasana, Lecturer, G.P. Women's College, Imphal.
5. Miss Ating Haokip, Chief of Saivom.
6. Miss Grace Satsang, President, Naga Women Union.
7. Miss Kim Gangte, Ex. M.P.

8. Mr. K. Prongo Keishing, Retired Government officer.

9. Mrs. Aman, Keubung Thawan.

10. Mrs. Aram Pamei.

11. Mrs. Chinthem Kipgen, I.A.S.

12. Mrs. Hoikhovei Kipgen, age 80 years.

13. Mrs. Joyshree Mutum, Lecturer, G.P. Women's College, Imphal (Department of Chemistry).

14. Mrs. Khanongla Keishing, 84 years. (Retd. School teacher), Bungpa village.

15. Mrs. Laljan Begum, Member, Manipur State Commission for Women.

16. Mrs. Lhingzaneng Gangte, Member, Manipur State Commission for Women.

17. Mrs. Nemneikim Vaiphei, Pastor, Kuki Baptist Church, Chassad Avenue, Imphal.

18. Noorjahan, Mema, President All Manipur Muslim Women's Development Organisation, Kairang.

19. O. Sumati Devi, Head of Department, Botany, G.P. Women's College.

20. Rani Chungkham.

21. Rev. Seikholet Singson, Age 80 years.

22. Rose Mangshi, Retired Lecturer, G.P. Women's College, Imphal.

23. Th. Bina Rani, Lecturer, G.P. Women's College, Imphal (Deptt. of Pol. Science).

24. Valley Rose, Editor "Aya daily" in Tangkhul.

(C) SECONDARY SOURCES

1. Adino Vitso, Customary Law and Women, Regency Publication, Delhi, 2003.

2. Ahmad N., Women in India. A.D.H. Publishing Corporation, New Delhi, 2003.

3. Aleaz Bonita, Emergent Women Mittal Publication, New Delhi, 59, 2005.

4. Ali Asghar Engineer, Impact of Civilization, Shipra Publication, Delhi, 2005.

5. Anand, V.K. Major, Nagaland in Transition. Associated Publishing House, New Delhi, 1967.

6. Anjali Bagive : Of Women Caste, Stree Publication, Calcutta, 1995.

7. Aswathi Bela, Women's Liberation and women's World Omsons Publication, New Delhi, 2002.

8. B.C. Allen: Naga Hills and Manipur (Socio Economic History) Gyan Publishing House, Delhi, 1981.

9. Basudeb Dutta Ray, Asok Kumar Ray, Dynamics of Power Relations in Tribal Societies North East India Om Publication, New Delhi, 2006.

10. Bertram Carey and Tuck H.N: The Chin Hills. Firman KLM Pvt. Ltd, Vol. I&II, Calcutta, 1976.

11. Brown R, Statistical Account of Manipur, K.M. Mittal Sands Karan Prakashak, 65F Anand Nagar, Delhi, 1950.

12. Chib, S.S. : Caste Tribe and Culture of India, Vol.8, North Eastern India. Ess Ess Publication, New Delhi, 1984.

13. Clerk, M.M.A. : Corner in India, American Baptist Publication Society, Philadelphia, 1967.

14. Constantine R : Manipur Maid of the Mountains, Lancer Publishers, New Delhi, 1981.

15. Das, R.K.Manipur Tribal Scene.

16. Datta Ray B Tribal Identity and Tension in North East India, Omson Publications, New Delhi, 1989.

17. Debi Renu Women of Assam, Omsons Publication, New Delhi, 1975.

18. Downs F.S. The Mighty Works of God, Christian Christian Literature Centre, Guwahati,1971.

19. Dr. Jamini, Nupigee Yakairol Rai Prabeena Bros, Imphal, 2001.

20. Dr. Ram, S. Women and Social Change Ajay Verma Common Wealth Publishers, New Delhi, 2004.

21. Dr. Zehol Lucy Women in Naga Society, Regency Publication, New Delhi, 1988.

22. Dun, E.W. Gazetter of Manipur Vivek Publishing House, Delhi, 1975.

23. Dutt, R.R., An Outline of world Vicilization New Delhi, 1965.

24. E.M. Rogers and FF Shoemaker (in) Communication of Innovatioin, A cross Cultural Approach New York, Free Press, 1971.

25. Elvin Varrier The Nagas in the nineteenth century Oxford University Press, 1969.

26. Furer Haimendorf C. Jon The naked Nagas, Mathew and Company, London, 1939.

27. Gangmumei K History of Manipur Vol. 1 Pre-Colonial Period, National Publishing House, New Delhi, 1991.

28. Gangte M. Priyadarshni Customary Laws of Meitei and Mizo Societies Akansha Publishing House, New Delhi, 2008.

29. Gangte, T.S. The Kukis of Manipur, Gyan Publishing House, New Delhi, 1998.

30. Ghose, G.K. & Ghose, Shukla, Women of Manipur APH Publishing Corporation, New Delhi, 1997.

31. Giri V Mohini, Emancipation and Empowerment of Women Gyan Publishing House, New Delhi, 1998.

32. Gougin T History of Zomi (first ed.) Printed and published by the Author, Churachandpur, 1984.

33. Grierson, G.A. Linguistic Survey of India, Tiobeto Burman Sub-Family (reprinted) Motilal Banarsedas, Delhi, 1904.

34. Grimwood E. St, C, My Three Years in Manipur, Vivek Publishing House, Delhi, 1995.

35. Haolai Thangkim Kuki Culture in North Cachar Hills Bohniman Printers, Guwahati, 2006.

36. Horam M.Ed. The Rising Manipur including North Eastern States Manas Publication, New Delhi, 2000.

37. Horam, M.Nagas Old Ways New Trends Cosmo Publications, New Delhi, 1988.

38. Hudson T.C. The Meitheis, B.R. Publishing, Delhi, 1975.

39. Jhalajit, R.K. A Shorot History of Manipur Imphal, 1965.

40. Johnstone J, Manipur and the Naga Hills, Cultural Publishing House, Delhi, 1993.

41. Kamei Gangmumei A History of Zeliangrong Nagas, Spectrum Publication, Guwahati, 2004.

42. Karam Manimohon Nupi Lan (Women's war of Manipur) Imphal, 2006.

43. Kaul Vinita, Women and the Wind of Change, Gyan Publishing House, Delhi, 2000.

44. Kh. Ratan Kumar Lai Haraoba of Manipur Imphal, 2001.

45. Kipgen Khaikhotinthang, The Thadou Kukis – A brief Account of History and Culture Swaaj Printing Press, Imphal, 1982.

46. Kipgen Mangkhosat, Christianity and Mizo Culture Assam Printing Works (P) Ltd., Mahatma Gandhi Road, Jorhat, 1996.

47. Ksh. Bimola Women's Movement in Manipur, Social Movement in Contemporary India K.K. Bagchi, Calcutta, 1998.

48. Lal Dena British Policy Towards Manipur (1891 – 1991) Churachandpur L & R Printing Press, 1984.

49. Lolly Rev. R.R. The Baptist Church in Manipur Modern Printers, Imphal, 1985.

50. M. Chandra (ed) Panthoibi Khongun Manipuri Sahitya Parishad, Imphal, 1999.

51. Mackenzie Alexander The North East Frontier of India, Mittal Publication, Reprinted, Delhi, 1979.

52. Mc Culloch M. Valley of Manipur, Gyan Publishing House, Delhi, 1980.

53. Medha Kunja (ed) Status of Women and Social Change, Women's Study Research Centre, Guwahati, 1996.

54. Meitei Y. Munan Bamon Khunthoklon.

55. Mills Moffatt A.J., Angami Life and Custom – The Nagas in the Nineteenth Century Virrier Elvin (ed.) Oxford University Press, London, 1969.

56. Misao P.C., History and Custom of the Thadou Kuki, Imphal.

57. Moghadan M. Valentine,Modernizing Women Gender and Social Change, Viva Books Pvt. Ltd., 2005.

58. N. Ibobi Manipuri Administration (1909-1907) Th. S. Manglem, Imphal, 1976.

59. N. Joy Kumar Social Movements in Manipur, Mittal Publications, New Delhi,1992.

60. National Research Centre, Meira Paibis, Imphal, 1999.

61. Paothing Free Z.V. Status of Tangkhul Women, Imphal.

62. Parratt Saroj Nalini and Parratt John The Religion of Manipur,Firma KLM Private Ltd., Calcutta, 1980.

63. Roy Kumkum (ed.) Women in Early Indian Societies, Manohar Publishers & Distributors, New Delhi, 2001.

64. Roy. S. Status of MuslimWomen in North India, B.R. Publishing Corporation, Delhi, 1979.

65. Sen Soumen (ed.) Women in Meghalaya, Omsons, New Delhi, 1997.

66. Shimray R.R. Origin and Culture of the Nagas, Samsoh Publication, New Delhi, 1985.

67. Shukla, Anil Kumar, Political Status of Women, APH Publishing Corporation, New Delhi, 2007.

68. Sircar Chaki Manjusri Feminism in a Traditional Society Shakti BNooks, New Delhi, 1984.

69. Sopitt C.A. A Short Account of Kuki Lushai Tribes on the North East Frontier. Firma KLM Private Ltd., Aizawl, 1976.

70. Thang L. B. The Mizos, A Study in Racial Personality, United Publishing, Guwahati, 1977.

71. Vumson, Zo History Aizawl, Mizoram, 1986.

72. Yunao Asoso Naga Struggle Against the British Rule Under Jadonang and Gaidinliu 1925-47 Kohima, Leno Printing Press, Kohima, 1982.

Index

A

Adult Franchise, 90
Agriculture practice in Nagas, 139
AIDS awareness, 159
Ancestor worship, 104
    Nagas, 143
Anglo Kuki War of independence, 91-92
    women role, 91-92
Animal sacrifices, 146
Animism in Nagas, 143
Armed personnel torture of women, 161
Arun, Prof M.C., 24
Awareness programmes
    Kuki women, 100

B

Banru ceremony Nagas, 145
Basil plant, 40
Bimolata (designer), 32
Blood connections Kukis, 83
Boy/girl differentiation, 27
Bride Price, 16, 84-85, 126
Brown, R., 30
Bubel Khur, 97
Buhfai Tham *see Handful of Rice Project*
Burial of Muslim Pangal women, 72

C

Chang Cha Kou ritual, 105
Chang-ai ceremony, 109
    role of women, 109
Change process, 74
Chon ritual, 106
Christianity, 110-11
    converts in Nagas, 149, 169
    impact, 150-51

in Kukis, 168
contribution to women, 115-16
Chumpha phanit festival, 144
Chung Kham Rani
contribution to weaving, 31
Chung Pathen *see God (Kuki)*
Church women's role in, 147
women's department, 148
attitude to women, 169
role, 116
Colonialism impact, 35
on women, 29
movement against, 35
Committee on Status of Women, 15
Communicable Diseases
Manipur, 157
Constitution of India, 16
Council of elders, 111
Court of women, 34
Crops cultivated by Kukis, 95-96, 98
Cross-cousin marriage Kukis, 84
Cultivation Nagas, 139

D

Dai-phu ritual, 106
Death ceremonies Kukis, 107
Death customs/rites of Kuki woman, 85
Muslim Pangal women, 72
Death in child birth, 136
Naga practice, 136
Death price Kukis, 83-84
Deities Nagas, 145
Democratization, 43
Departing Ceremony (death), 144
Directive Principles, 16
Divorce, 16
in Muslims, 58
Dormitories, 130
Dowry system in Meiteis, 27
Dress Kuki women, 81
Dumphol *see Tobacco leaves*

E

Economic condition, 69
Education, 69
Nagas, 141
and Muslim women, 55
in Meitei Pangal, 74
Elections women participants, 37
reserved seats for women, 38
Elite women of Manipur, 28
Environmental degradation, 160
Ethnic Communities Manipur, 80

F

Famine in Manipur, 36
and women's movement, 36
Feast of Merit (death), 144
Female guardianship, 20
infanticide, 27

Feminism in a Traditional Society, 17
Festivals Kukis, 105
Five Year Plans and women's issues, 156
Fund raising by Kuki women, 112

G

Gambih tour *see Preaching Tours*
Gangte, Lhingjaneng, 82, 84, 90-91
Gangte, Ms Kim, 91
Garibaniwaza, King temple destruction by, 40
Gender functions, 44
    differences, 52
    interest safeguarding of, 74
Gender Sensitive Intervention, 161
Genna, 146
God (Kukis), 102
Government Programmes for women & child health, 156

H

Haimendorf, 127
Hanafi law, 73
Handful of Rice Project, 112
Haosa *see Village Chief*
Head hunting, 107
Health Care Institutions in Manipur, 157
Health Policies of Government, 158
Hinduism impact on women, 24, 27
    in Manipur, 39
Hindu-Muslim relations, 52
Hiram ceremony, 59
HIV Prevalence State, 159
Hoijakim Mrs, 93
    as spy for INA, 93
Holy female, 41
Hospitality of Nagas impact, 141-42
Human Rights, 137
Hun ceremony, 105
Husband's death rites
    Nagas, 144

I

Illiteracy, 17
Income and expenditure, 67
Indian National Army
    Kukis in, 92-93
Indoi Religion of Kukis, 103-105
Inter village wars in Nagas, 128
Irengba, King, 51
Islam tenets of, 70
    religious lessons in, 71
Islam entry in India, 61

J

Jai Singh King rule, 40
    daughter's role, 40

Jhum cultivation, 95
Johnstone, J., 126

K

Kabui Naga women political participation,133
Kabui Nagas Womens role, 145
Keithei Marup system at, 30
Khagemba, King, 50-51
  rebellion, 51
Khankam, 82
Kho-geh ritual, 106
Kho-Thempu *see Village priest*
Khutlang organisation, 29
Khutsup Anchang *see Handful of Rice Project*
Khwairamband Market, 30, 68
Kinship, 110
Kithumpuba *see Holy female*
Kuchu organisation, 34
  divisions, 34
Kuki Baptist Convention, 114
Kuki Chief, 87
  powers, 88
  house, 88
Kuki Chin, 80
Kuki Christian Church, 111-12
  role of women, 113
Kuki customs, 94
  economy, 99
  socio-economic life, 99
  language, 111
  society change, 116
  men work of, 98
  ministers, 87
  Rebellion, 93
  Sporting Club, 101
Kuki woman, 80, 168
  role, 79-82, 89
  role in.. economy, 94-96
  agriculture, 95
  sports, 101-102
  religion,102, 168
  church,168
  economy, 96
  rallies, 86
  politics, 87
  history, 80
  as weavers, 96
  dress, 96
  in Parliamentary elections, 91
  women work of, 98
  as bread earners, 100
  death customs, 85
  role appearance, 80
  dress, 81
  voting, 90
  ornaments, 81
  hairstyle, 81
  position, 81-82
  chieftains, 89-90
Kukis, 79
  freedom struggle, 92
  origin, 80
  changes in, 86
  society, 82-83
  patriarchy, 83

L

Labour force of women, 167
Lai Haraoba, 43
Lairobi, Sija Princess, 40
Lamkhoneng, Mrs, Haokip, 90
Language and literature, 111
LOM group, 167
London School of Oriental and African Studies documents, 50
Longman custom, 168

M

Macrae, John, 87
Maibis, 44-45
  Meitis, 42
  women as, 42
  dress, 42-43
Male-female mixing, 27
Manipur ethnic communities, 80
Manipuri Muslims clan, 50-52
  arrival, 51
  history, 51
Mao Nagas God, 144
  Rice Plantation ceremony, 145
Maram society practices in, 136
  unwanted laws, 136
Marriage system of Kukis, 84
Marup system types, 29
Mate, Mrs Vahjaneng, 90
M-bong Katai practice *see Death in child birth*
McCulloch, Col, 49, 80
Meira Paibis role playing, 25-26
Meitei Pangal Society
  changes, 73
  women, 74
Meitei- Pangal women, 18, 62, 166
  role, 49, 60,62,165
  in religion, 70
  in politics, 61, 167
  in economy, 65
  status, 73, 165
  position, 53
  rights, 55
  death rites, 72
  education, 55, 60, 74, 166
  and health, 60
Meitei Pangals, 53
  Socio-economic survey 2004, 66
Meitei women and politics, 33
  economic role, 17, 28
  status, 16
  education, 17
  role, 23-24
  bravery, 25
  motherly role, 26
Meitei on, 59
Moirang INA in, 94
Morung *see Youth Chambers*
Mosque entry issue of women, 71-72
Motherly role, 26

Mothers seat, 127
Muftias training, 72
Mungyamba, King, 51
Muslim marriage, 57
    taboos, 57
    celebrations, 58-59
    widow remarriage, 57
    divorce, 58
    customary functions, 58
Muslim Pangal women, 53
    lifestyle, 53
Muslim women %age, 67-68
    and religion, 70, 72
Muslim Women organizations/
    movements, 62-63
Muslims socio-economic
    scenario, 63-64
My Three Years in Manipur, 23
Mysticism, 43-45

N

Naga rites and sacrifices, 146
    word, 123
    area, 123
    appeareance, 124
    tribes, 124
    society, 125
    society changes, 141-42
Naga women, 169
    activities, 140
    source of income, 140
    emancipation, 142
    role, 125-26
    as wife status, 127
    in war, 129
    in politics, 132
    in economy, 138-39
    occupation, 126
    inheritance, 126
    appearance, 126-27
    talents, 130
    restrictions, 131
    spy role, 131
    perception of, 131
    uplift, 150
    organisation, 135
Naga Women's Union Manipur,
    137
    objects, 138
    claims, 137-38
Nagas Western lifestyle, 149
    Christianity adoption, 149
    converts, 149
Neutral lady, 129
NSCN-IM ethnic cleansing
    impact of, 100

O

Occupational hazards, 160
Ordination, 150
    of women, 114
Ornaments Kuki women, 81

P

Pacha Loishang, 29
Paddy cultivation, 139
    Field rituals, 144

Paite women position of, 82
Panchayati Raj System, 91
Pangal (Muslims) socio-
  economic survey, 56
  women position, 53
  education, 55
  rights, 55
  population, 49
  social structure, 53
  customs, 54
Pangal society changes, 73
Panuka Puba ceremony, 59
Parliamentary Elections
  Kuki women in, 91
Pastors, 115, 148
  women as, 148
Patriarchal society Nagas, 148
  Pangals, 54
  Kukis, 83
Patriarchal woman, 85
Pei Hinga, Queen, 136
  reformations by, 136
Personal law reforms, 74
Political activities role of Muslim
  women in, 61
Politics and women, 19-20, 34-35
Population census 2001, 65
Preaching tours by women, 113
Pre-Colonial period, 15
Pre-wedding celebrations in
  Muslims, 58-59
Priestesses in Kukis, 108
Priesthood and Shaminism, 44
Priests *see Maibi*
  Prophet's wifes, 62
Protests by women, 63
Pukhareila *see Neutral lady*
Pundit Loishang, 43
Purdah system, 73, 166

Q

Quadir Mirza Fazlul, 50

R

Rasa dance, 40
Reforms, 74
Religion Naga, 143
  and Meitei Pangal women,
    70, 72
  Meitis, 39
  division, 39
Religious lessons Islam, 71
Remarriage in Muslims, 57
Restrictions, 69
Rice beer, 97, 110
Rice Plantation ceremony Mao
  Nagas, 145
Rituals women's role in, 147
Rongmei Tribe, 124

S

Sa-ai ritual, 105
Sadhika *see Holy female*
Sagei Kwa Yenba ceremony, 58
Salt making, 50
Samong Pachong *see Council of
  elders*
Sanongba rebellion by, 51
  POWs, 52

Sanskritic rituals, 41
Sanskritisation, 28
Sati instances of, 27
Scarcity syndrome, 19
Semang Pachong, 88
Senapati District, 124
Seven Years devastation -
    period, 28
    women during, 35
Sharma, B Kulachandra, 50
Spirituality of women, 19
Structural interventions, 161
Sun-gao relative, 83

T

Tangkhul tribe, 124, 133
    famous women, 133
Thadou women position, 81
The Chin Hills, 80
Tobacco juice, 97-98
    leaves, 97
    smoking, 97-98
Trade and commerce Kukis, 99
Tribal Society, 16
Tucha Sungao relationship in
    Kukis, 83
Tuibuh *see Tobacco juice*

U

Umnit/ Sahnit observance by
    Kukis, 106
Universal Adult Franchise, 36-
    37
    and Kukis, 90
Universal Brotherhood, 73

V

Vaishnavism rise of, 40
    culture, 41-42
Village Authority Act Manipur,
    89
Village Chief, 111
Village Council, 90
Village priest, 108
Violence against women, 158-59
Voting women in, 37
    rights of women, 134

W

War and devastation impact on
    women, 28
Weaving, 31-32
    Naga women, 140
    Kuki women, 96-97
    women in, 31
    vendor-weaver relations, 32
    shops, 33
Western education impact, 99
Wet Cultivation Field gift to
    Naga daughter, 142
Widow remarriage, 16, 57
    in Nagas, 126
Woman Pastors, 149
Women occupational hazards,
    160
    concerns, 160-61
    and politics, 19-20, 33

Women (contd)
avenues choices, 29
occupation, 33
court, 34
education, 17, 71
mosque entry, 71-72
Muslim, 53
religious role, 38, 41-42, 45
as Maibi, 42
status, 16-17, 68-69
role played, 18-20, 69
different communities, 20, 23
fellowship, 111-12
Women chieftains Kukis, 168
Women health, 155-56
interventions
suggestions, 162
Government programmes, 156
in Muslim history, 61-62
market categories, 30
Ordination of, 114
Working women, 17
Wrestling, 131
Writing skills encouraging, 137

Y

Youth Chambers, 130

Z

Zeliangrong Naga, 128
famous women of, 133